THE

# AGONY

## OF

# AFFLUENCE

CANTILEVER BOOKS are a response to the need for making the data of scholarship acessible to the nonspecialist. Like the cantilever bridge, which, supported at each end, is built from both ends toward the middle, each book in the imprint seeks to bridge the gap between the author's knowledge and the reader's natural curiosity. Cantilever Books make it possible for the reader to explore and to "fall in love with" a new subject, a new discipline, a new perspective, a new pursuit.

# THE
# AG$ONY
## OF
# AFFLUENCE

## WILLIAM W. WELLS

CANTILEVER BOOKS
Zondervan Publishing House
Grand Rapids, Michigan

THE AGONY OF AFFLUENCE
Copyright © 1989 by William W. Wells

Cantilever Books is an imprint of Zondervan Publishing House, 1415 Lake Drive, S.E., Grand Rapids, Michigan 49506.

**Library of Congress Cataloging in Publication Data**

Wells, William W., 1943-
    The agony of affluence.
    Bibliography: p.
    Includes index.
    1. Wealth–Religious aspects–Christianity.   2. Wealth
–Biblical teaching.   3. Wealth, Ethics of.   4. Economics
–History–20th century.   I. Title.
BR115.W4W43    1988          241'.68          88-28054
ISBN 0-310-21761-X

All Scripture quotations, unless otherwise noted, are taken from the HOLY BIBLE: NEW INTERNATIONAL VERSION (North American Edition). Copyright © 1973, 1978, 1984, by the International Bible Society. Used by permission of Zondervan Bible Publishers.

Peanuts cartoon reprinted by permission of UFS, Inc.

*Edited by Judith Markham*
*Designed by Jan M. Ortiz*

*Printed in the United States of America*

89  90  91  92  93  94 / PP / 10  9  8  7  6  5  4  3  2  1

*To David, Eric, and Brian.*
*My prayer for each of you is that God will give you his blessing throughout life, and perhaps even prosperity. But I also pray that God will give you his grace so that you will know how to live with such a blessing.*

# CONTENTS

# PART I
# A FOUNDATION

# 1
# Facing the Dilemma

"There is no way out," Kent Hartford concluded. "No matter how I resolve this, someone is going to disapprove."

The land was not the problem. That was an inheritance from an uncle. Getting the money was not the problem. Kent was a partner in a prosperous law firm. The problem was nothing as relatively straightforward as money or land. The problem was this: In a world where one billion people go to bed hungry each night, did Kent, a Christian, have a right to build a vacation home for his family?

Kent's pastor had taken a strong stance on the matter. Christians should not, he argued, spend their money on luxuries while there were still people in the world going hungry. Sarah Downs, a Christian colleague in his law firm, disagreed vehemently; she considered Kent's scruples unjustified in light of his clear commitment to both the church and the work of the kingdom of God. For example, their law firm allowed them to spend up to ten percent of their time on "charity" cases for which there would be no income. Out of concern for the poor, Kent regularly used his quota of time. Furthermore, he consistently and generously supported the work of his church with both his time and his money.

Kent's wife understood both sides clearly and had concluded that they should build a vacation home. Kent's profession placed him under a great deal of pressure and stress, and limited his time with the children. She believed that building a place where Kent could unwind on the weekends and where they could spend their vacations together as a family was an appropriate use of a portion of their money. But she had assured Kent that she did not want to begin building unless he felt right about it. So the final decision rested on his shoulders and conscience.[1]

Living with personal prosperity, yet wanting to please God by making responsible and moral economic decisions in a world full of human need: that is the agony of affluence. But what do I mean by affluence?

Do I mean men in perfectly coordinated Ralph Lauren shirts and slacks working their golf handicaps down at a posh resort? Or perhaps diamond-ringed, gracefully aging women flitting between their spas, club luncheons, and theater openings? Certainly these are some of the images of affluence in our culture. Yet in a worldwide context and by any reasonable standard, you and I are wealthy. We are both educated; I am able to write, and you are able to read. We both have leisure time to pursue these and other activities.

Or let's look at our wealth in another way. Suppose the word *wealthy* means that you have more than your *fair* share. Again, measured by the average income worldwide, we both probably have more than our share. You may think that definition is too broad, and I agree. It tends to destroy the concept of a middle class, making everyone either wealthy or poor. So let's modify the standard somewhat and say that the *wealthy* are those who have annual incomes in the top 20 percent worldwide. Again, on a worldwide standard, we are probably both wealthy.[2]

For the duration of this book, then, let's see ourselves honestly in relation to the rest of the world and admit that we are affluent; and let's admit that this affluence raises two sets of questions that could create some agonizing dilemmas for us.

First of all, why do we have this wealth? Where did it come from? Is it ethical to possess this wealth? Is there an inevitable link between wealth and oppression? These questions focus on a search for truth, and we will need to draw information from both Scripture and economics in order to answer them.

Second, what should we do with our wealth? Some biblical passages seem to suggest that God expects us to give it away. Does he expect us to give *all* our wealth away? Or can we keep some? Can we save some for our retirement? At what point does our appreciation of the good things God has given us become materialism? How can we recognize when we have accepted the moral and ethical standards of our culture? Is a "Christian capitalist" a contradiction in terms?

Some evangelical writers assert: "If you are wealthy, you are guilty of injustice. You should, therefore, give it all away now." Other Christians point to the Old Testament promises of wealth and prosperity to the faithful, claiming that we can enjoy the wealth of this world.

Most evangelicals find themselves somewhere in the middle, dissatisfied with both extremes, yet lacking the biblical or intellectual framework that would provide an alternative. In this book I would like to provide you with the beginning of just such a framework.

In doing this, I will sidestep political issues, even though economics and politics are closely related. Economics studies how the actions of individuals in the marketplace establish prices and how government decisions affect the business environment. Political science studies the structure that we use to govern ourselves and the responsibilities and freedoms of citizens. The two are logically distinct, however, and this book is primarily about economic issues.

Some Christian thinkers seem unable to distinguish between the two. They find the political repression in Chile so offensive, for example, that they simply cannot look at the economic policies of Pinochet's government without bias. Jim Wallis's book *Agenda for Biblical People* suffered from this fault. His concerns were appropriate, but he painted with too wide a brush, failing to separate political and economic issues.[3]

In other cases, the anguish of personal involvement blurs the distinction. Bonganjola Goba, a black South African, writes,

> I live in Alexandria Township, perhaps one of the most filthy places in this country, with no proper infrastructure, a place which stinks because we still have the old bucket system. But a few kilometers away from where I live, we are surrounded by the beautiful clean white suburbs of Kew, Lombardy East, Sandton, and Wynberg. Living in this terrible situation of squalor is a testimony of how the economy of this country is designed to consolidate and to protect white economic interests. It makes a mockery of the virtues of the so-called free-market system. For in the eyes of blacks, the free-market system represents a powerful instrument used by the white political system to perpetuate capitalist exploitation.[4]

In context it is abundantly clear that Goba is taking a stance not against capitalism, but against the repressive South African political system. A casual reader, however, could take his impassioned words as a critique of free-market policies.

I will assume throughout this book that one can distinguish between economics and politics. This is a practical decision. It does not mean that I approve of the economic policies of repressive governments. For our purposes here, however, I simply need to isolate the religious/economic issues raised by affluence from other closely related issues.

Another caveat is necessary. Even limiting the affluence issue to matters of the religious and economic, I cannot possibly deal thoroughly with the topic in this short book. Rather, I am suggesting an agenda and framework for discussion of these questions. Although I will not mention them frequently, I will be in constant dialogue with books such as Ron Sider's *Rich Christians in an Age of Hunger,* with the wealth-and-prosperity school, and with Gary North's Institute for Christian Economics, probably best presented in David Chilton's *Productive Christians in an Age of Guilt Manipulators.* Those who are interested will find a critique of these positions in the appendix.

Part I examines the patterns of biblical thought that unify the Bible. In contrast, Part II looks specifically at modern economics from a business perspective, examining only those ideas that contribute to solving issues raised in Part I. And Part III attempts to bring the evidence from both of these sources together into an ethical synthesis.

# 2
# Biblical Interpretation

About fifteen minutes after school normally began, the door opened and my son Eric walked into the house. His teacher had sent him home because he was barefoot.

It was early September and our family was just beginning a sabbatical year in southern California after spending six years in Hawaii. In the Aloha State it is perfectly acceptable for children to wear flip-flops to school, or even to go barefoot. Southern California was different.

In spite of Eric's confusion and perplexity at being sent home, the basic rule had not changed: clothing standards are set by the school. But the context had changed, and in southern California shoes are required. Eric just had not yet realized that the new school had its own set of rules.

The Bible, too, has a context. When God spoke his word, he always spoke into a specific time and place. So if we wish to hear the message of Scripture correctly, we need to know something about that context. In recent years, Bible scholars have used the term *contextualization* to describe attempts at bridging the cultural and temporal distance between biblical times and today. These scholars claim that proper interpretation begins by trying to understand the significance of the biblical teaching and commandments in the time and place in which they were written. Contextualization is the process of then expressing the meaning and significance of those passages in terms of twentieth century culture, language, and thought.[1]

This interpretive process has a second dimension. We must not only move from the ancient culture to the present; we must also move from the specific to the general. Originally God's Word came to specific people in specific situations. Today, those who proclaim God's Word from the pulpit help us understand these same texts and apply their specific meaning to our lives. Our interpretive task here, however, is not tied so closely to specific texts. Rather, we must generalize from many passages, and we must reason by analogy. In so doing, we will be constructing a biblical theology, a generalized statement of what God was saying in all the specific details.

Let me illustrate the complexity of this interpretive process. In the Jubilee Year, land was returned to its original owners (Lev. 25:8–17). Ron Sider argues that this practice was an attempt to keep the economic gulf between the rich and the poor from becoming an unbridgeable chasm.[2] He is probably right. But how does that apply today? What is our economic equivalent? If we want to contextualize the Jubilee today, what would we return? And furthermore, how do we deal with other related specifics that the Bible doesn't address? For example, why was land returned in the Jubilee Year but not the houses inside walled villages?

Or consider another biblical mandate: Farmers were prohibited from harvesting their fields to the edges, or from going back and picking up grain that was dropped. They were required to leave these "gleanings" for the

poor (Lev. 19:9–10; 23:22; Deut. 24:19–22; Ruth 2:1–9).
What is the twentieth century equivalent of gleaning? In
our urban society, how can those who are wealthy share
appropriately with those who are not?

The Old Testament prohibits charging interest on
loans. But how does that apply today? Corporations are
legal entities recognized by our society, yet they have only
existed during the last one hundred years or so. The Old
Testament knows nothing of such capitalistic economic
structures. Hence the Bible cannot possibly speak directly
to the question, "Should a corporation be allowed to pay
interest to an individual?" If we want to discuss the ethics
of interest in a capitalistic society, we have to reason from
limited evidence.

Scripture provides a great deal of data, but it does not
speak to some issues directly. The theology of the biblical
writers is bound up, almost inextricably, with an ancient
cultural context that provided specific commandments for
an ancient people. It does not provide general principles
that can be applied to twentieth century issues. If we wish
to formulate these general principles, we must somehow
ourselves bridge the theological chasm from the ancient
period to the modern and move from such specific
commands to generalized economic conclusions for today. Don't expect quick answers. The economic teachings
of Scripture cannot simply be imposed on the twentieth
century. They must be contextualized, and that is one of
the primary tasks of this book.

I am not the first to attempt this task, of course. From
the beginning, the church has struggled with such matters. But in attempting this interpretive process, the
church has tended to fall into two extremes: asceticism
and worldliness. The former tendency was aggravated by
gnosticism, a Greek philosophy which asserted that
matter—the physical stuff of our world—is inherently
evil. The truly pious person, according to gnosticism,
recognizes the world for what it is: an enticement to
debauchery and evil. Such a person shuns physical reality

whenever possible. Some gnostics, for example, advocated celibacy, and all of them taught austerity as a general norm.

The early church recognized that such a doctrine did not square with the Christian faith. The Creation and the Incarnation, for example, are clearly incompatible with it. Nonetheless, this bent toward asceticism flowed into the church through early monasticism.

Worldliness, the opposite extreme, appears whenever Christians forget the rigorous demands of the gospel. The bishop/princes of the Middle Ages probably represent this error most clearly. Called by God to lead the church, they embroiled themselves in the political problems of their day and neglected their religious responsibilities. Often they had access to tremendous wealth, and many neglected their responsibilities and settled in to enjoy the good life.

Today, these extremes still exist, and advocates of each believe they know how to deal with affluence. In both cases, much of what they say is a fair reflection of the biblical perspective. But their lack of balance forces me to reject their conclusions. The search for a biblical theology of wealth and prosperity will involve balancing such extremes.

# 3
# Wealth in the Biblical Perspective

The Bible begins with a wonderful picture: an exuberant God creating a bountiful world filled with fruitful vegetation, animals, and waters teeming with fish. When his world was complete, God created a man and a woman and placed them in the midst of this abundant world. All creation was theirs.

As he gave them this gift, God commanded Adam and Eve to be fruitful themselves, to multiply, and to care for his creation. In Genesis 1 and 2 it is absolutely clear that God intended Adam and Eve to enjoy his creation and that it would supply their needs completely.

When God appointed the first man and woman to be stewards of his garden, he wanted them not only to care for it, but to bring order to it and make use of it for their needs. "Subdue the earth," he said. "Rule over the fish, the birds, and every living creature. Every seed-bearing plant . . . every tree . . . will be yours for food." Just read the first two chapters of Genesis and note the bounty of God's gift. God provided abundantly for Adam and Eve. They in turn were to live in obedience to God's com-

Charles M. Schulz *Peanuts Treasury* reprinted by permission of UFS, Inc.

mandments. In so doing Adam and Eve could create wealth for themselves.

In Eden, wealth obviously had little to do with bank accounts. The point was not accumulation, but enjoyment and proper use of the creation God had provided. The land would produce abundantly. Wealth would be the natural result of the good stewardship of that first couple.

A biblical theology of wealth and prosperity must rest on the basic doctrine of creation. And in formulating that theology, we must look at both the nature and purpose of God's creation and at our role as stewards of that creation.

## The Nature of God's Creation

At the conclusion of each of the days of creation, God announced his approval of his work. He expressed particular approval after creating mankind on the last day. They, he noted with pleasure, were very good *indeed*.

But this idyllic state did not last, for Satan entered the scene. Since then, evil (sin) has been disrupting and corrupting our world at every point. God's creation did not become evil, but it could be used for evil. In fact *everything* in the created order now has this capacity.

Even the abundance God has provided can be used for evil. It can tempt us to idolize material things, and when this happens, the pursuit of wealth becomes our master. Because of this, wealth must be treated with great care. The warning that it can enslave us runs throughout Scripture.

The Old Testament says that wealth can be a blessing, a gift from God. Yet the prophets condemn those who allow it to lure them into oppression. In the New Testament Jesus warns, "You cannot serve both God and Money" (Matt. 6:24).

The Gospels tell us of a rich young man who came to Jesus and asked what he had to do to inherit eternal life. Jesus told the man to sell everything he had and give to the poor and follow him; then his true treasure would be in heaven. On hearing this, the young man walked away sadly. His attachment to his worldly goods was stronger than his desire for salvation. His wealth had become his god, an occasion for evil (Luke 18:18–23).

In his letter to the Romans, Paul explains that humanity began worshiping creation rather than the Creator when they took their eyes off God. Whereas men and women were intended to exercise dominion over creation, they became enslaved by it (Rom. 1). In Ephesians and Colossians, Paul pictures the principalities and powers of darkness that strive to dominate humanity.

Wealth is one of those powers: it attempts to exert control over us.

In spite of the incredible disruption that evil brought into the world Scripture nowhere teaches that creation itself became evil. God's creation is still good! I cannot overemphasize this point; it is an essential premise for the theological perspective articulated in this book.

Furthermore, God has not left his creation mired in evil. The New Testament teaches that a day will come when evil will be judged by God and the earth itself will be destroyed. Then, just as he redeemed us through the sacrifice of his Son, God promises to conclude history by creating a new heaven and a new earth. In this final act, he will show his fundamental commitment to his creation. Creation may be in bondage today, but God has plans for its redemption.

We must not, therefore, allow the presence of evil within creation to cause us to disdain it. Though cursed, it remains good and we are free to celebrate its beauty and its bounty. Any theology that denies this joy and celebration is flawed.

## God's Purpose for His Creation

When evil entered the world, it disrupted and corrupted God's creation. But evil could not alter God's purpose for his creation nor can it can deprive creation of its value. God intends for his creation to bring us joy and to provide for our needs completely. So whenever God redeems his people, he fulfills his purpose for creation, which includes celebration, joy, and abundance.

When God liberated the people of Israel from their Egyptian rulers, he promised them "a land flowing with milk and honey" (Exod. 3:8). Later, in the desert at Sinai, he offered the formal covenant that promised such physical blessings as crops, cattle, and even children (Deut. 7:13–15). But because God offered his covenant to a people who had already fallen away from him, he also threatened to withhold blessing from those who disobeyed and broke the covenant.

God must deal with evil, but that necessity should not obscure his readiness to bless. Again and again the Old Testament displays God's commitment and desire to bestow blessings upon his people.

The New Testament abounds with similar images of prosperity and abundance. While attending a wedding in the town of Cana, Jesus was confronted with a simple but embarrassing problem. The host had run out of wine. As his first public miracle, Jesus turned the water in six stone pots into wine. Archaeological evidence from the period shows that those stone jars, used for storing water for the household, probably contained twenty-five or thirty gallons each. That means that Jesus provided approximately six hundred quarts of wine for that wedding. God intends us to use what he created to celebrate life's important moments.

In another New Testament story, Jesus miraculously provided food for over five thousand people. He not only fed the crowd; he provided enough for leftovers! "Just enough" was not enough. Abundance was his standard.

The Gospels record the fact that the Pharisees charged Jesus with being a glutton and a drunkard. There is nothing to support their charge, but the fact that they made it at all suggests that Jesus attended banquets and enjoyed parties with his friends. Jesus was not an ascetic. A theology that views God as stingy or mean fails to take into account his creation and actions while on earth.

Future events also maintain this. The marriage feast of the lamb, one of the key biblical images of eternal bliss, is clearly an image of abundance; and the Book of Revelation describes the city of God as a city paved with gold.

We must not underestimate God's desire to bestow good things—literally "things"—on us. Nor can we allow the disruption of evil to deprive us of our desire—legitimate and good—to enjoy the delights of creation.

God wants to supply our needs abundantly as his purpose for his creation continues.

## God's Purpose for Us

In 1970 I received an invitation to teach at the University of Hawaii, which allowed my family to live in a state filled with the abundance of creation. Yet that abundance in itself did not create wealth. When driving around the island, we often passed vast quantities of guava rotting by the roadside. Only when human creativity and energy in the form of a guava juice industry captures some of that abundance does the natural bounty of the land become a source of wealth and human satisfaction. In creating that industry and using that natural abundance, the people of Hawaii contribute both to their own enjoyment of the world and to the enjoyment of those who live elsewhere and would not normally have access to the delicious tropical guava.

This pattern seems to be a part of the created order: proper stewardship of God's abundance creates wealth to be enjoyed.

This distinction between abundance and wealth is fundamental. God provides abundantly, but we create the wealth through our hands, our imagination, our ingenuity, our abilities, and our hard work. God has called us to take an active role in bringing order to our world and, in so doing, to provide our own wealth and prosperity.

Here again, however, we see the effects of evil. For along with disrupting God's creation, evil disrupts our ability to act as his stewards and affects us in two distinct ways.

First, evil disrupts and thwarts our best efforts at bringing order into the world. The Genesis narrative pictures man prior to the Fall naming the animals and tending the garden—Adam, the gentleman farmer. But after the Fall, labor became source of frustration and even despair.

This despair was etched on the memories of many farmers in the Depression of the 1930s. During that time prices fell, and farmers suffered along with the rest of the population. Some of the farmers concluded that they could bring prices back up by creating artificial shortages, and so they began to burn their own crops. The land had produced, but society had not been able to turn that abundance into prosperity. The evil that had permeated the structures of society broke out in economic distortion. Without evil, such a travesty would never have occurred.

Second, the presence of evil in our world interrupts our work and thrusts two new tasks upon us. These new tasks stand continually in conflict with our original task of creating wealth from God's abundance.

God did not create poverty, yet Jesus told us that the poor would always be among us. This fact confronts the godly with an insoluble problem: the Old Testament assumes that each person will be productive and that the community will thus have its needs amply supplied. Each of us is to be productive so that all can share in and enjoy the results. Yet since the Fall, the prosperous can no longer simply enjoy their wealth; they are commanded to feed the poor. They are called to devote part of their time and energy to aiding others who, because of the distortions introduced by evil, will not or cannot provide for themselves. Caring for the poor is, then, the first of the two new tasks that compete with our original task.

The second new task results from the fact that good and evil are now at war within our world. The people of God are called to the proclamation of the gospel. Jesus Christ provided a prime example. At the Incarnation he set aside the natural wealth he had as the Son of God and became a servant (Phil. 2). Jesus commanded his disciples to follow his example (Luke 14:33).

In this second task, Christians are faced with another insoluble problem. We are given a task for which we are not suited. We were simply not created to fight evil. But because evil has invaded our world, God has called us to join him in the fight. And that task pulls us from our original task of providing for our material needs from God's abundant creation.

In short, evil has introduced complex problems into our lives. We must deal with economic distortions that cause human suffering and we must carry out our economic tasks in tension with two other new tasks. Yet we must not allow the presence of evil to tempt us to retreat from, or demean, our original responsibility—the task of bringing order to God's world and in so doing creating wealth from God's abundant creation. Furthermore, the symmetry of God's work suggests that in the final restoration our stewardship will be renewed.

As Charlie Brown remarks in the cartoon at the beginning of this chapter, "Sound theology has a way of taking a load off our minds!" In dealing with the agony of affluence, a sound theology can allay both our vague anxieties and our guilt. The natural abundance of our world can be perceived as a burden. A sound theology can transform that burden into a gift and enable us to use that abundance with generosity and thanksgiving rather than with selfishness and greed.

In the midst of the evil of this present world, we need the solid foundation of a biblical perspective on wealth and poverty, justice and injustice, consumption and sharing. Our culture often legislates against this, of course, and our own personal sin can lead us to destroy each other in the pursuit of wealth.

Because of this, those who find wealth too great a temptation may have to pass up some opportunities to enjoy it lest they worship it rather than the Creator. Furthermore, God may call some individuals to give up their enjoyment of the abundance he created in order to serve others. For them, the task itself will dictate a simple life-style. But, in the end, we are free to receive wealth as God's gift to the extent that we are capable of receiving it.

# PART II
# MODERN ECONOMICS

# 4
# Economic Interpretation

There is no such thing as a married bachelor; the term is meaningless. But how about Christian capitalists? Do they exist? Certainly there are many people who claim to be that. But are they? Are Christianity and capitalism compatible? Can one be both a Christian and a capitalist?

A number of evangelical Christians believe that no Christian could possibly be a serious capitalist and that no "right wing" capitalist could be a "real" Christian. Those who are truly Christian, they say, give away their worldly goods to help the poor; capitalists only want to amass greater and greater wealth for themselves and the elite. Yet many other evangelicals feel just the opposite. Christian and capitalist fit naturally together. The business world depends on capitalists—people who have power and can control substantial amounts of money. Why shouldn't Christians work comfortably in such a system for the betterment of the world?

These two groups find it difficult to even discuss matters of wealth from their opposing viewpoints, and when they try, they often go away perplexed, frustrated, and even angry with each other. It's a classic case of poor communication. Both groups think they are debating theology and ethics when in reality they are arguing from dual assumptions: scriptural and economic. Neither group realizes, usually, that their arguments rest largely on their undiscussed economic assumptions.

Is it legitimate to build a theology on a source outside the Bible? Is it even possible to integrate biblical theology and economics? This issue is key to the theological and ethical questions raised by this book.

## Integration

God revealed himself to us in Scripture, and by studying it, we learn about him. God also commanded us to exercise stewardship over his creation, and that, too, entails study and understanding. Since God took the initiative in both cases, we must assume that his self-revelation and his creation are consistent with each other. God is not, after all, in conflict with himself.

Both revelation and creation, however, must be interpreted to be understood. For example, if we see a conflict between Scripture and science, the problem must be with us. We ar mistaken in either our biblical interpretation or our scientific interpretation. The problem is *our interpretation*. We err gravely when we assume that the proper interpretation of either God's revelation or our world is obvious. Interpretations are open to change as we learn more. Consider this reminder from history.

Galileo built the first telescope and used it to explore the sky. He was surprised to see that the planet Jupiter had moons. At that time the scientific community was sharply divided over the question of whether or not the Earth was the center of the universe. Galileo's discovery that Jupiter had moons showed conclusively that Earth was not the one, unique center of the universe. Jupiter's moons, at least, did not orbit Earth.

The church, however, disagreed. The Book of

Joshua, they pointed out, said that the sun stood still for the people of Israel during a key battle in the conquest of Canaan. That implied, they argued, that the sun normally moved around the Earth and that therefore the Earth was the center of the universe. Since Galileo's conclusions were in conflict with Scripture, he was wrong and a heretic. Galileo suggested that his accusers look through his telescope, but they refused to do so. Scripture, they insisted, was clear on the point. It was not up for debate.

Today, of course, we acknowledge the fact that the Earth orbits the sun, and we interpret the passage in Joshua in other ways. We have, in short, allowed our growing knowledge of the world to shed light on our interpretation of Scripture. In Galileo's case, a scientific discovery altered the accepted interpretation of Scripture, and the Christian community changed the way it read Scripture.

It is important to point out, however, that intellectual influence moves in both directions. The Bible can also modify widely accepted but incorrect scientific interpretations. The biblical record has, for example, corrected archaeology on occasion and later been "vindicated" by further scientific research.

In Scripture we are commanded to love each other, but it takes practical knowledge about our personal world to obey that command. We learn how to love members of our family by listening to them as they express their needs, wants, desires, and dreams. We can then reflect on what we have heard in the light of Scripture and begin to love effectively.

Sometimes, however, we need to pursue truth about the physical world around us in a more rigorous way if we are to care for others effectively. For example, doctors use their knowledge about how the body works to decide on the proper medical treatment that will restore us to health. But in some cases, doctors find themselves with no good options: ultimately, they cannot prevent death. Thus, at times their knowledge may allow them only to minimize suffering and provide the best possible care under the circumstances.

Economics has the same potential. It may be an imprecise science at best, but economics has been able to clarify the ways human beings trade goods and services with each other. It can, therefore, help us understand how to care for each other more effectively in the economic realm.

Unfortunately the science of economics has limitations much like medicine. There are occasions when economists must offer advice in a situation where there are no good options—no matter what they advise, someone will suffer. The responsibility of the economists, then, is to recommend policies that will best serve the needs of all people, and particularly the needs of the poor. Just as a physician must sometimes prescribe remedies that themselves cause pain or discomfort (chemotherapy, for instance), the economist must sometimes recommend such things as austerity.

A Christian view of affluence must take into account both God's revelation as recorded in Scripture and the science of economics. As I examine the economic options available to us, I will generally take a conservative, pro-capitalist approach. Taking such a position is not simply a preference for one economic theory over another. I believe these conclusions allow us to care for the poor most effectively.

## Economic Issues

Every society must accomplish two economic tasks: (1) it must produce goods and services, and (2) it must distribute them to consumers. These tasks in turn raise two questions: (1) How should society structure its economy to encourage efficient production? (2) How should a society encourage just distribution of those goods and services?

Many socially concerned evangelicals ignore the first

question and jump directly to the question of just distribution. This mistake does the poor a great disservice. If society could double production without altering the existing patterns of distribution, it could double the goods and services given to the poor! Theological and ethical reflections on affluence must examine both the creation of wealth and its just distribution. Economic analysis can make an important contribution to our understanding.

Broadly speaking, the field of economics can be divided into macroeconomics and microeconomics. The first deals with the impact of the government's fiscal policy (taxes and the money supply), patterns and levels of employment, and measures of the health of the economy (inflation and economic growth). As the prefix "macro" implies, it looks at the larger picture, the structure of an economic system. Microeconomics, on the other hand, looks at a narrower set of issues. It studies how prices are set.

Macroeconomics is as controversial as theology. And, like theology, there are various schools of thought. Microeconomics is *substantially* less controversial. Economists may, for example, agree on how the price of wheat is set but disagree vehemently about whether the government should subsidize farm production.

In the following pages we will in general ignore macroeconomics. Most of us have no control over those factors in any case. Microeconomic analysis, in contrast, can illuminate situations where we do in fact make practical economic decisions that address the problem of poverty and hunger.

# 5
# Origins of Wealth and Prosperity

The "Prairie Home Companion," Garrison Keillor's delightful and popular radio show, comes from the mythical town of Lake Woebegone, a place where all the children are "above average." A place where everyone is above average is, of course, nonsense. But a place where everyone is prosperous is not.

So far we have used the word "abundance" to signify the natural productivity available to us in God's creation and the word "wealth" to describe what we create from that natural abundance. I have suggested that we use "the wealthy" to refer to those who own or control enough wealth so that their annual income is in the top 20 percent of the world's population. Although this is an arbitrary definition, for the purposes of this discussion it helps us gain a perspective on our own economic situation.

At this point, however, we need to add "prosperous" to designate people who have enough resources to meet all their genuine physical needs: that is, they have adequate food, clothing, and shelter; access to medical and dental care; and opportunity for at least a high school education.

It is not logically possible for everyone to be wealthy; not everyone can be in the top twenty percent. But it *is* logically possible for everyone to be prosperous. It is also technologically possible for the first time in the history of the world.

## The Creation of Wealth

Most people assume that the total amount of wealth in the world is fixed and that the wealthy are simply people who manage to accumulate "more than their share." This assumption has profoundly influenced evangelical social commentary in the last two decades, as evidenced by the following quotations from well-known Christians who have addressed the subject.

> Private accumulation, however, is unreservedly and remorselessly condemned [in the Bible], because it can only take place at the expense of others.[1]
>
> Our overconsumption is theft from the poor.[2]
>
> We have abruptly awakened to a new image of our planet as not only a finite but a shrinking pie.[3]

But wealth is not a fixed, never-changing amount. Economists agree that wealth can be created. For Christians who want to live responsibly with affluence, this fact has astonishing and profound implications. At the very least, it should change the questions we ask, as Michael Novak articulates well.

> Most sociologists write articles about "the causes of poverty." They are asking the wrong question. . . . Poverty is the natural condition of human beings. Poverty is what you have when you do not know causes. The question is not, what causes poverty, the question is how do you create wealth?[4]

Between 1500 and 1776 most of the European nation-states believed the amount of wealth in the world was fixed, static. It seemed to be a "limited good." In economic discussions, a limited good is often called a "zero sum game." (Where a limited good exists, the gain of one individual is always at the expense of another. A pie is such a limited good. If one person takes more than his share, then someone else's piece must be smaller. In a zero sum game, the gain of one person—a positive—will always be offset by the loss of another—a negative. The sum of the gains and the losses will be zero.)

These European states viewed international wealth as a zero sum game: the success of one country had to come at the expense of another country. The wealth of one country meant the poverty of another.

Furthermore, those early nation-states were committed to their own financial growth and prosperity and, by implication, to the economic decline of their neighbors. This led to two specific practices. First, they tended to hoard gold and silver. Second, they discouraged imports and encouraged exports. Imports drained gold from their national coffers since they had to pay for the goods, while selling exports increased their gold. Thus, the European nations of that period were committed to national policies based on the idea that import tariffs and beggar-thy-neighbor practices would produce wealth for their own countries. The premises underlying these policies were called *mercantilism*.

Then in 1776 Adam Smith challenged the basic premises of mercantilism when he published *The Wealth of Nations*. He denied the idea that wealth is a zero sum game and advocated the revolutionary idea that wealth can be created whenever the work force of a nation specializes. Division of labor is the key, he said.

> A workman not educated to . . . the trade of the pin-maker . . . nor acquainted with the use of the machinery employed in it . . . could scarce, perhaps, with his utmost industry, make one pin in a day, and

certainly could not make twenty. But in the way in which this business is now carried on, not only the whole work is a peculiar trade, but it is divided into a number of branches, of which the greater part are likewise peculiar trades. One man draws out the wire, another straights it, a third cuts it, a fourth points it, a fifth grinds it at the top for receiving the head; to make the head requires two or three distinct operations; to put it on, is a peculiar business, to whiten the pins is another; it is even a trade by itself to put them into the paper; and the important business of making a pin is, in this manner, divided into about eighteen distinct operations which, in some manufactories, are all performed by distinct hands, though in others the same man will sometimes perform two or three of them. I have seen a small manufactory of this kind where ten men only were employed, and where . . . each person . . . [averaged] four thousand eight hundred pins in a day. But if they had all wrought separately and independently, and without any of them having been educated to this peculiar business, they certainly could not each of them make twenty, perhaps not one pin in a day.[5]

Smith denied the common assumption that precious metals constituted a nation's wealth. He asserted, in contrast, that national wealth was properly measured by the annual produce of the land and labor of the country. Increased productivity was the key to increased prosperity.[6]

If this is the case, then division of labor and specialization become one source of increased productivity and wealth. Scientific and technological advance and its application to production provide a second major source.

When I left teaching some years ago, I began working in a large commercial bank as a financial analyst. At one point I was asked to use a variety of assumptions to project the size, financial structure, and profitability of the bank for the next five years. I did the work with a calculator and handwritten work sheets. My electronic calculator made the work substantially easier than it would have been a decade ago, but it still took me almost a month to complete the project.

Six months later I gained access to a personal computer and learned to use an electronic spread sheet. Within days I had become proficient enough with these new tools to replicate a month's work in less than a week! Adopting this new technology increased my productivity, lowered the cost of preparing such an analysis and increased, even in a small way, the bank's profitability. Such shifts to a higher technology have occurred multiple times in the United States during the last decades, and each has contributed to our growing wealth.

Technological advancement raises an important question however. When a technological breakthrough occurs, company owners are usually willing to invest money to purchase better technology, for in so doing they increase their own profits. But how does the hourly employee get his or her share of that increased productivity? Surprisingly, the answer is rather straightforward.

As profits in a business sector rise, investors tend to pour money into that sector. Eventually this influx of capital enables the business to satisfy consumer demand; competition follows, and prices fall. When this happens, everyone—including employees—benefit from lower prices. For example, I could not afford to pay $250 for a hand-held calculator in the early seventies. But demand for calculators was high and electronics companies invested heavily to improve quality and lower prices. Today one of those small calculators costs about $10, and even grade school children use them. Because they are so inexpensive, we forget the tremendous contribution calculators have made to our productivity and consequently to our wealth.

Technological advance not only creates wealth, however, it also creates disruption, for new technology often replaces labor. And this fact raises a second question: How can we justify displacing workers?

The answer is not difficult in the abstract, although it certainly causes pain to those involved. While workers are being forced out of one area because of technological advance, new opportunities are being created in other areas where displaced workers can find new jobs. Such moves subject workers and their families to the pain of change. Displacement may call for retraining and perhaps even relocating, but that is the price of industrial growth. To those involved, it is a painful price. The alternative, however, is a stagnant, dying economy.

As banks began to use computers during the last few decades, thousands of bookkeepers who manually tracked checking and savings accounts were displaced. Yet while destroying certain jobs in the banking industry, the adoption of computers created other jobs. For example, the use of credit cards would have been impossibly expensive a generation ago. Today, the credit card industry uses the services of those same bookkeepers who were originally displaced by the computer. So while computer technology did destroy jobs, it also opened up opportunities in industries created by the application of that technology. And while the transition undoubtedly caused pain for some people, the new services available today benefit us all.

Wealth can be created. And as the total "pie" to be divided grows, our ability to care for the poor also grows. Enhanced productivity is, therefore, essential in enabling us to deal with poverty and hunger. This leads us to the second proposition of this chapter.

### Three Influences on Production

The "physical fallacy," says Paul Johnson, is "the assumption . . . [that] any kind of middleman or non-producer is an obnoxious parasite."[7] This assumption is basic to Marx's theory of value, and governments who hold to it undermine the production of wealth through their social policy. Johnson provides a classic illustration.

I was made aware of the consequences of the physical fallacy when I visited Indonesia in the twilight of the obnoxious Sukarno regime. Sukarno, a socialist and a racist, had persecuted the minority Chinese business community to the point that it was no longer able to function. As a result, in the capital of Djakarta there was virtually nothing to eat. Less than 100 miles away, as I saw for myself, villages were producing fruit, vegetables and meat in abundance, and it was rotting unsold. The Chinese traders who ran the trucks which carried the food from villages to the capital had been hounded off the scene, and no one had yet been able to take their place. So the market system did not function.[8]

But governmental action can also encourage the production of wealth. China has traditionally found it difficult to feed its entire population. In 1979, the Chinese government began to experiment with a variety of capitalist incentives in its farm sector. Five years later *The Wall Street Journal* (November 2, 1984) featured an article entitled "China, Awash in Grain Becomes a Big Exporter" which stated that the "successful policy of allowing families to operate private plots" was the significant factor in China's producing a bumper harvest.

Cultural factors are equally significant in affecting productivity. In *The Spirit of Democratic Capitalism,* Michael Novak points out that North America and Latin America stood on roughly equal footing in the mid-nineteenth century. The economic differences that have developed since that time are a direct response to the differing cultural values of the two continents. The United States has become the wealthiest country in the world while South American countries like Argentina teeter on the verge of bankruptcy.

Latin Americans do not value the same moral qualities North Americans do. The two cultures see the world quite differently. Latin Americans seem to feel inferior to North Americans in practical matters, but superior in spiritual ones. . . . The "Catholic" aristocratic ethic of Latin America places more emphasis on luck, heroism, status, and *figura* than the relatively "Protestant" ethic of North America, which values diligent work, steadfast regularity, and the responsible seizure of opportunity. Between two such different ways of looking at the world, intense love-hate relations are bound to develop. . . . As Latin Americans do not admire Northern virtues, North Americans do not entirely approve of Latin virtues.[9]

In the Third World, many cultures hold the zero sum premise and are thus skeptical of the value of wealth-producing activities. Their stagnant economics bear testimony to their mistake. In contrast, those Third World cultures that believe wealth can be created encourage it where possible.

Even when cultural factors are similar, though, the economic structures of nations may differ. And these economic structures are crucial in encouraging or discouraging production. This becomes evident when we compare countries with similar social and historical roots but different economic structures.

Compare, for example, Ivory Coast and Ghana. Ivory Coast, with its capitalist structure, has a growing economy, whereas Ghana, its socialist neighbor, is one of the poorest countries in the world. The relatively impoverished economy of North Korea compared with the dynamic economy of South Korea is another example of different economic structures. Compare also the economic growth of Taiwan since the Chinese revolution in 1948 with the production of mainland China since that time, as well as the productivity of Austria with that of Czechoslovakia.

The *1983 Report on World Development* published by the World Bank explored the relationship between economic policies and development in the Third World. The message of the report was clear. Countries that produce

price distortion through governmental action discourage
economic growth and increase the likelihood of poverty.

> Economic achievement and progress depend largely
> on human aptitudes and attitudes, on social and
> political institutions and arrangements which derive
> from these, on historical experience, and to a lesser
> extent on external contacts, market opportunities and
> on natural resources. And if these factors favorable to
> material progress are present, persons, groups and
> even societies will not stagnate. . . .

> If all conditions for development other than capital
> are present, capital will soon be generated locally, or
> will be available to the government or to private
> businesses on commercial terms from abroad, the
> capital to be serviced out of higher tax revenues or
> from the profits of enterprise. If, however, the
> conditions for development are not present, then
> aid—which in these circumstances will be the only
> source of external capital—will be necessarily unpro-
> ductive and therefore ineffective. Thus, if the main-
> springs of development are present, material progress
> will occur even without foreign aid. If they are
> absent, it will not occur even with aid.[10]

This brings us to a crucial question in dealing with
affluence: If governmental, cultural, and economic factors
combine to encourage productivity, what, then, are the
sources of American productivity and prosperity?

## America's Prosperity and Third World Poverty

Thirty years ago, Reinhold Niebuhr wrote of America's prosperity:

> This wealth is a tremendous hazard to our moral
> prestige throughout the world. It not only tempts
> others to envy, but gives a certain plausibility to the
> communist charge of "capitalist exploitation." This
> charge is not well-founded because our wealth does
> not even depend upon a great percentage of foreign
> trade. We have a more nearly self-sufficient continen-

tal economy than any other nation. Our wealth is due primarily to the high degree of efficiency of our techniques and of our whole industrial enterprise.[11]

Much has changed in the intervening generation, but Niebuhr's basic point is still valid: U.S. wealth is not the result of exploitation, but of efficient production. Only 5 percent of total U.S. investment is made in foreign countries, and only 7 percent of its production is exported.[12] In fact, there is mounting evidence that imports are now draining wealth from the U.S. economy.

Furthermore, U.S. international investments go primarily to developed countries, not developing countries, and U.S. trade is shifting increasingly toward developed countries. In 1962, 51 percent of U.S. exports went to developing countries. By 1980, only 40 percent went to those same ports.[13] Some critics claim that U.S. trade with Third World countries is inherently exploitive. The evidence, however, does not bear this out. The poorest areas of the world are those that don't trade with the West.[14]

Nor do these charges deal with historical evidence. In the mid-nineteenth century, Latin America and the United States were roughly comparable economically. Since then, the United States has pulled ahead because of the Anglo-American commitment to progress. "Although Brazil is apparently one of the most richly endowed of all nations in material resources, neither Brazil or other Latin American nations have so far provided a system favorable to invention and discovery."[15]

Some also argue that Western wealth was extracted from former colonies, but again the evidence says otherwise. "Some of the most backward countries never were colonies, as for instance Afghanistan, Tibet, Nepal, Liberia. . . . At the present one of the few remaining European colonies is Hong Kong—whose prosperity and progress should be familiar." The United States, Canada, New Zealand, and Australia were originally colonies and have become prosperous in spite of that colonial heritage.[16]

All this raises the obvious question, "Why do people persist in believing that the wealth of the United States is based on exploitation?"

First of all, much that we hear from church pulpits seriously misrepresents reality. For example, we are frequently bombarded with statements like, "6 percent of the people own 50 percent of the phones in the world." While factually true, such contentions are also half-truths. In the case above, the same 6 percent who own 50 percent of the phones also manufactured 60 percent of the phones in the world. Such assertions carry little more than shock value, and certainly do not address the real question, "Why are the 6 percent so productive?"[17]

Second, the perception that the wealth of the U.S. is ill-gotten gain is often the result of fuzzy thinking. Paul Simon writes, for example, "In 1974 more than half of the grain that entered world export markets flowed from the United States. In this respect our control of grain exports is similar to the control over oil exports that countries of the Middle East exercise."[18] Yet the comparison is ludicrous. Oil is a mineral that exists in some places and not in others. Countries with ample oil deposits have wielded great economic power in the last decade. Grain, on the other hand, is grown by those who choose to cultivate it. Therefore, it should be obvious that the United States cannot control the worldwide production of grain. Furthermore, the U.S. has neither formed nor participated in a cartel with other major grain producers to limit production and raise prices.

And finally, the zero sum game concept discussed above provides a third source of this misunderstanding about U.S. prosperity. We will have to take a specific but hypothetical example in order to see how this concept perpetuates such misunderstanding.

Suppose a multinational corporation invests $100 million in a Third World country and that over the next ten years this new business returns $10 million a year in profits to the United States. Those who argue that the United States exploits Third World countries will claim that additional profits returned to the United States after the ten-year period amount to exploitation of the people of that Third World country. Since $100 million was invested, only $100 million should be returned. Any further withdrawal amounts to exploitation.

Consider this, though: First, that $100 million investment created wealth within the Third World country by creating new employment for nationals. Second, the $10 million return per year is a fair annual return on an investment—it's only 10 percent a year. If the zero sum game premise were true, returning additional profits to the United States would indeed be unjust, but it is not. The original investment in plant and equipment continues to exist, and the workers continue to want employment. Consequently, the company can continue to operate. Thus, the original investment will continue to generate wages for the national workers and a justifiable 10 percent return to the investor who made it all possible. The productive combination of capital and labor will continue to generate wealth.

Government action, cultural factors, and economic structures have made the U.S. tremendously productive. That does not mean this country is without fault; some U.S. businesses do violate the demands of justice. But in general, the wealth of America is not the booty of an unjust society. U.S. prosperity is made in America.

Prosperity and wealth can be created. That discovery is at the core of modern industrial society, and those countries that have structured their economies to encourage productivity are enjoying increased wealth and decreased human suffering. By implication, then, increased productivity is fundamentally more important in dealing with world poverty and hunger than attempts to equalize distribution.

# 6
# Alternative Economic Systems: An Introduction

As I walked away from the house, images of people I had met in recent weeks and memories of conversations flooded my mind. With them came a series of profoundly disturbing questions.

It was the summer after my freshman year in college, and I had decided to spend it selling books in the farm communities of central Illinois. During the course of that summer I had met elderly people living on limited incomes and farmhands skirting the edge of poverty. In the house I had just visited, I had met a young couple who received a house, some food, and a very small income in return for the husband's work as a farmhand. It was obvious to me that he and his wife were on their way to becoming just like many of the elderly couples I had encountered, living out their last years with no savings and little means of support.

I had been reared in a conservative family where I was taught the value of individual initiative. Now, however, I was meeting people who seemed either unable or unwilling to take responsibility for their own economic well-being in the present or the future. For the first time I was facing questions related to the social responsibility of government.

What is the proper role of the government? Should it merely organize an economic system and let it take its course, or is the government responsible to intervene on behalf of some of its citizens? When its citizens' wage-earning years are over, is a government responsible for their economic needs in their retirement? If people—young or old—are either negligent or unable to afford medical insurance, is the government responsible to make this provision?

As a society, we profess two sometimes conflicting economic values: the first is efficiency and the second is justice. Efficiency is associated with production. The more efficiently we produce goods and services, the more we as a nation have to consume. Societies that do not put a premium on efficiency simply produce less, even though they may start with the same materials and use the same number of man-hours. Such countries are typically plagued with shortages and often with famine.

Justice is the standard associated with the distribution of good and services. An economic system that allows for too great a disparity between the rich and the poor cannot be tolerated. Nor can a system that allows the rich to use their economic power to oppress the poor.

Unfortunately, these two values interfere with each other in our fallen world. If the former is emphasized too much, society becomes cold and heartless—like the efficiency expert who lays people off work without ever considering what that measure means to the individuals and their families. On the other hand, in nations where just distribution is more valued than efficiency, economic activity seems to slow and even die.

It does little good to say, "There ought to be a better way," if the best economic thinkers do not know of a better way. Thus, we must first look at the existing economic structures available to us. How efficient are they? How does the creation of wealth fare under various structures? And, how just are these structures?

Economic systems fall into three broad categories: (1) barter systems where people trade goods and services with each other directly; (2) traditional economic systems that use money but function at a preindustrial level; and (3) modern economic systems.

Although some Christian thinkers idealize the simple life-style, they do not seriously suggest that we abandon the use of money. We can, therefore, ignore the barter system. Neither do they suggest that we should give up the productivity created by industrialization, which is beginning in the Third World as many countries slowly move toward industrialization. So traditional economic systems need not concern us here.[1]

Perhaps I should emphasize that this chapter is not simply a survey of possible economic systems. Rather, we are asking, "How *should* a modern economic system be structured?" The options fall into two broad categories based on the answer to one central question: Given the fact that goods and services are limited at any particular point in time, how should we allocate them among all of the people clamoring for them?

The market system, or capitalism, answers this question by saying that we should not even try to allocate goods and services. Rather, we should allow the rise and fall of prices for goods and services and our collective response to those fluctuations determine who gets what. By its very nature, then, capitalism is fragmented and impersonal, its course determined by the law of supply and demand.

Command economies, or socialism, offer a second and entirely different answer. Socialists believe that individuals should decide how to allocate goods and services. Command economies are therefore inherently centralized, planned economies. Typically, a government agency tries to carry out the task of planning, and, by implication, the government must own the means of production.

Thus, one point is clear already. The market system rests on an impersonal, fragmented foundation: on price levels and more fundamentally on the law of supply and demand. Centralized economic systems, in contrast, are based on a personal foundation: on human decision.

Christianity, it is important to note, is not a third option. The question "How should we allocate goods and services?" is an economic question. Christianity does not have an alternative to those two choices. Christians too must answer the question, "Should we allow prices—by themselves—to allocate goods and services appropriately? Or should people intervene at some point? And, if so, to what extent?"

Furthermore, Christianity does not *clearly* teach one particular economic system.[2] Instead, it offers a value system for evaluating the process by which economies are implemented and how well they produce and distribute goods and services. Consequently, there are Christian capitalists and Christian socialists. The latter tend to argue that the market system does not care for people adequately, and hence they call for centralized planning. The former often point out that the poor fare better under capitalist systems than under planned economies, particularly in developing countries. But as Christian capitalists and Christian socialists discuss and debate, they are not offering alternative Christian solutions; they are offering Christian reasons for preferring one system over the other.

## Market Economies

Let's begin by looking at a simple problem and its solution within the market system.[3] Traditionally, Americans barbecue both steaks and hamburgers during the summer. Many of us prefer steak, but hamburger is less expensive, so we have to decide how often to treat ourselves to steaks. The attached graph provides a simplified picture of how we as a nation make this decision.

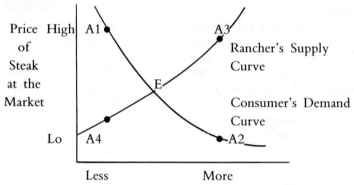

The Quantity of Steak Available

The vertical distance on the graph is the price of steak. The horizontal axis indicates the number of steaks we will want to barbecue this summer and the amount of steak ranchers will bring to market. The line from A1 to A2 is called a demand curve. It shows how much steak we as consumers will demand at various prices. If the price is high (A1), we will consume less. If it is low (A2), we will consume more. The line from A3 to A4 is called a supply curve. It shows how much steak will be brought to market at various prices. It indicates that farmers and ranchers are willing to supply more steaks to the market when the price is higher (A3) and less when the price is lower (A4). The point where the two lines cross (E) indicates the equilibrium point: a price and quantity that balances supply and demand. In less technical terms, the equilibrium point is a price at which consumers are willing to buy exactly the amount of steak that ranchers are willing to sell.

Occasionally, production gets out of balance with consumption. When ranchers believe that prices will be high, they increase production. If they overestimate demand and produce too much, prices have to fall to encourage consumers to buy the additional meat; when that happens, ranchers experience economic hardship. When the opposite happens, they produce too little. In this case, they can raise prices and still sell all of the meat that they have on hand. Consumers may complain, but someone buys it all anyway.

Note, however, that there is no villain in either case. Rather, the market moved away from its equilibrium position temporarily. Furthermore—and this is the basic assumption of the market system—the market can be expected to return to an equilibrium. If there is not enough steak and prices rise above the equilibrium point, farmers and ranchers will respond by raising more cattle, which will bring prices down. Conversely, when prices fall, they will produce less, and the prices will go up again. The market (that is, all of us acting as a corporate whole) will correct the problem. No one—more specifically, no *agency*—needs to interfere with this process.

We as individuals make our various choices. Then prices, as they are set by the impersonal forces of the law of supply and demand, communicate information about our needs and wants to the market. When prices of a commodity are high, the market is signaling the need for more of that commodity. And when the reverse is true, low prices signal a glut of a commodity.[4]

By implication—and note this carefully—there is no inherently "fair" price for steak. The price we can expect to pay in the store this summer is simply a price that will equate the demand of consumers with the supply of producers.

When we stop talking about steaks and begin talking about the demand for labor, we find this has profound ethical implications. Let's look at the issues as they are graphically related in John Steinbeck's *The Grapes of Wrath,* a book that caused some stir at its publication.

The story takes place during the dust bowl era in the

United States when migrant workers began moving westward hoping to find employment in the citrus fields of California. Wages were low, living conditions poor, and some of the farm workers were agitating for union representation. Management, of course, opposed unionization. Steinbeck helps his readers see this conflict from the viewpoint of a migrant family.

On first reading, one almost inevitably sides with the laborers who simply want a living wage. That seems like a reasonable request. Yet the economist, at the risk of seeming totally heartless, must raise more fundamental questions and examine all of the factors contributing to the situation.

Low wages are a signal that the labor market is out of equilibrium. In the story, too many workers were applying for too few jobs. In such a situation, raising wages will allow those with a job to live better, but it will do nothing whatsoever for those standing outside the gate wanting a job. The economist will likely recommend that some of the laborers move on to other areas of the country where more jobs are available.

Unemployment and low wages are a signal to the labor community that some of its members will have to continue moving. There are simply too many people seeking too few jobs. Unemployment is like pain in the human body, unpleasant but necessary. It signals the need to respond. A compassionate person may feel deeply for the anguish of those workers, but compassion alone does not create jobs, nor does raising wages.

In the earlier example, both the price of steak and the quantity delivered to the market could change if necessary to reestablish equilibrium. In other cases, the supply of a commodity is inherently limited. (There are only so many seats on the fifty-yard line at the Rose Bowl.) When the quantity is fixed, prices must operate alone to bring the market to equilibrium. The same holds for people with specialized skills, such as musicians, athletes, and entrepreneurs. Since their abilities are relatively rare, they tend to be more highly paid than those people possessing relatively common skills. At first this may seem unfair, but it is inherent to the market system. "However we might wish it otherwise, it simply is not possible to use prices to transmit information and provide an incentive to act on that information without using prices also to affect, even if not completely determine, the distribution of income."[5]

*The Grapes of Wrath* takes place during the depression of the 1930s which compounded the problem for the migrant workers. The labor market was encouraging them to move on when there may not have been anywhere to move to. Throughout the United States there were too many people and too few jobs. Nonetheless, the basic point stands: raising wages will not create more jobs for the unemployed.

The key question is this: How are jobs created? How can more employment be created to absorb those workers?

The market system permits owners to keep their profits. Owners, of course, hope for even greater profits; and in the process of pursuing this goal they often expand their business, thus creating more jobs. If owners could not keep some portion of their profits, there would be no growth and no new jobs.[6]

When thinking about the wealth of the United States and the poverty of some Third World countries, it is helpful to remember the diagram above, for international economics works much the same way. The prices of commodities are set as the market moves toward a balance between supply and demand. As the price of bananas rises, for example, Americans will consume fewer bananas. We may grieve over the poverty of Central American peasants who work the banana plantations for a pittance, but simplistic solutions that demand they be paid more may not work. Higher wages would have to be passed on in the price of bananas, and if the price of bananas rises, consumers buy fewer bananas. As a result, plantation workers would have less work and could even lose their jobs.

Or let's take a positive example of the market system causing higher wages. In the late 1950s the computer industry was just beginning, with no precedents set for employment opportunities or wage scales. Out of 110 million workers available at the time, how many should have moved into the emerging industry and how much should they have been paid? The answer provided by the market system was this: allow prices to determine supply and demand. And it worked. As demand grew, wages went up and people were drawn into the industry. Profits increased and new firms entered the scene. In the end, the computer industry thrived.

Within the market system, the government can take on a fairly wide range of roles. In *laissez-faire capitalism,* which was more characteristic of the United States in the nineteenth century, the government understood its role to be minimal. It established the legal system within which the economy worked, but the economy was left pretty much to itself.

By the mid-twentieth century the market system in the United States could more properly be referred to as *guided capitalism.* Capitalism is guided when the government intervenes in certain ways to support what it values and, in some instances, to protect the weak. For example, the government does not set the price of housing, but the government has influenced the price of housing by allowing us to deduct our home mortgage interest on our income tax returns. In the recent past the government encouraged investment by taxing long-term capital gains at a lower rate than ordinary income, and it has encouraged domestic oil production in the interest of national security by providing favorable tax benefits to investors in that sector of the economy.

Countries to the "left" of the United States but still clearly aligned with the West—Sweden and Holland for example—are sometimes called socialist. In fact, they should be termed *welfare state capitalism*. In these countries the government levies high taxes in order to create—it is hoped—greater social welfare. Nonetheless, virtually all of the means of production continue to be owned by private individuals, and prices still play a major role in the economy.[7]

The differences among these three versions of capitalism lead to distinctly different social policies. For example, during his presidency Ronald Reagan argued strongly that the high tax rates characteristic of welfare state capitalism discouraged productivity and undermined the long term welfare of the whole society. More liberal politicians contended that the government had potential for doing good. Yet both sides had to admit that the evidence for either was not conclusive. Both sides would agree, however, that such differences are minor modifications of a basic market system. And both sides are worlds removed intellectually from those who advocate command economies, to which we now turn.

## Command Economies

Michael Novak points out that "traditional societies are aimed against disorder. Socialist societies are aimed against inequality. Democratic capitalist societies are aimed against tyranny."[8] As we have seen, market economies allow the impersonal forces of the market to allocate goods and services in order to maintain personal freedom. In contrast, command economies allow economic decisions to be made by the government in order to distribute goods and services with greater equality. The government may make these decisions through its agencies, or it may delegate responsibility to specific individuals. But in the end, the government decides what wages should be paid for various jobs, how much items will sell for in the store, and which items will be produced.[9]

As we saw in the previous chapter, capitalism was implemented in some Western European countries toward the end of the eighteenth century. Some observers, however, did not like the new economic order. The market economy was often whimsical and capitalism allowed a vast discrepancy between the wealthy and the poor. Those early observers concluded that capitalism not only did not, but could not, produce a society that would measure up to their understanding of justice and that only economic planning could improve the situation.

The idea of socialism as an alternative economic system became widely discussed during the first half of the nineteenth century. Its advocates believed that a planned economy could produce a more just society than could an unfettered market economy. Just as prices and the market system are at the core of capitalism, central planning and ownership are at the core of socialism. Its advocates consciously chose to forego some freedom for the sake of greater equality.

I remember watching a television interview of the leader of a Third World country. Asked about freedom in his country, he replied, "Freedom is a luxury. We must limit freedom in order to create a social order which is capable of providing adequate food for *all* of our people." Advocates of socialism do not deny that capitalism produces more goods and services. But, they claim, just distribution is more important than abundance; the wealthy must forego abundance for the sake of the poor.

Several visionary groups with strong leaders tried to implement socialism in the United States during the nineteenth century, but their efforts died out within a generation or two. The strong leadership of the founders seems to have been essential to their success. And indeed, Karl Marx argued that such benign versions of socialism were doomed to failure because they lacked a clear philosophical basis.

*Communism,* Marx's version of socialism, rests on a distinct philosophy of history: that is, history is moving inevitably toward the goal of a classless society that will embody the egalitarian socialist vision.[10] Its proponents hold that the suppression of freedom is a temporary but necessary stage on the way to that classless society. They would acknowledge that communism today is totalitarian, but they would insist that the totalitarian state is not a permanent characteristic of communism.

One element of the communist economic system deserves particular attention, however. Communist economic theory holds to the "labor theory of value." This theory states that all economic value is created by human labor, which is embodied in the goods and services that are the product of that labor. The laborer, therefore, has the right to the value he produced. If he is defrauded of the product of his labor, those responsible are guilty of *exploitation*.[11]

Let me explain: Suppose that a group of friends pool their resources and build a small manufacturing plant. They hire a management team, workers for the plant, a sales force, and begin to market their wares. After several years, the business flourishes and the owners are able to begin drawing dividends from their business. The communist theoretician would argue that withdrawing dividends is exploitation. After all, he would say, none of the owners produced anything. By withdrawing surplus profits, the owners are in effect stealing the labor embodied in the goods produced by the laborers. Owners, or capitalists, are therefore inherently unjust because they inevitably exploit workers.

The labor theory of value is an essential element in the philosophical foundation of the communist theory of exploitation and is at the heart of its fundamental opposition to capitalism. However, the theory is advocated only within Marxist circles and is explicitly rejected by virtually all contemporary non-Marxist economists. Outside of communist circles, economists recognize that capital, management, and technology also contribute to creating value, which explains why owners, managers, and inventors should also be paid.

Christian critics of guided capitalism occasionally use

the term *exploitation* without acknowledging its ideological roots in Marxist theory or giving it an alternative definition.[12] Since I know of no other meaning of the term, I avoid using it or responding to the charge. We should be concerned with the biblical concept of *justice,* rather than *exploitation* with its Marxist overtones.

These two systems, then, are the only real economic alternatives available today. Capitalist societies depend upon the market to make some of the most fundamental social choices. Socialist societies delegate these choices to the government. And since there is no third, Christian alternative, we must evaluate these two systems in light of biblical injunctions. Which economic system can create the most "appropriate" balance between the need for efficient production and just distribution?

# 7
# Alternative Economic Systems: An Evaluation

In evaluating socialism and capitalism, as presented in the previous chapter, we must remember one important fact: these two economic systems do not exist in a pure form anywhere.

Governments within capitalist countries like the United States operate businesses that could be turned over to the private sector. For example, where I live now, the city picks up my trash. A private company performed this function where I used to live. Given the logic of capitalism all cities should give this function to the private sector. Why should the city government be involved in the waste management industry?

Socialist governments often allow private industry to continue as long as it remains small. Most communist countries permit private citizens to sell produce from their gardens, for example. Given the logic of a socialist economic system, the government should absorb such privately owned businesses, but they do not.

Because both capitalist and socialist economic systems mix public and private ownership, evidence on how effective they are is sometimes difficult to assess. Nonetheless, the evidence on one point is crystal clear: if profits can be made in an activity, the private sector will perform that activity more efficiently than the government.

In every case where we can pair a capitalist country and a communist country, the capitalist country provides for its people better. The Western European countries have out performed the Eastern European countries by every economic measure since the end of World War II. Similarly, Taiwan has out performed mainland China since the communist revolution; and South Korea has out performed North Korea since the Korean conflict.

The World Bank report for 1983 provides a less intuitive, but statistically more reliable argument. Those who prepared the report developed an index to measure price distortion introduced into the economy by government intervention. Then this distortion index was correlated with the growth in the Gross Domestic Product from 1970 through 1980. The evidence was clear. The more a government intervened in the economy, the slower the economy grew.[1]

Why should this be so? First, as we saw in the previous chapter, business depends upon information about costs and opportunities, and prices convey that information. When the government intervenes, prices are set at least partially for political reasons. In so doing the government destroys the market mechanism that informs society about its collective needs and wants. Without this information, government operated businesses simply cannot run well. Second, when wages are set by government decision rather than as a reflection of productivity, individual initiative is decreased and productivity declines.[2]

In chapter 4 we raised two questions: 1) How can a society encourage efficient production? and 2) How should society encourage just distribution? If we focused only on the first question, there would not even be a debate. Capitalism would be the clear choice, for it encourages efficient production whereas socialism does not. But what about just distribution? Should we, on other grounds, choose socialism? Is just distribution more important than efficiency?

## A Theological Evaluation of Socialism and Capitalism

Capitalism's most fundamental weakness is this: It can recognize only economic values. It is blind to other values. For example, under capitalism the economic value of our labor is the contribution it makes to production. This contribution is measured by the salary an employer is willing to pay for it. But how do you determine the economic value of a pastor? A salary is a measure of economic value contributed. Since a pastor's contribution to his church is not usually economic, it cannot be measured that way.

Or, what is the value of the arts to a society? How much are they worth? Some economists would insist that they are worth whatever society is willing to pay for them. But that position ignores the rather simple fact that there are many values in this world, and they cannot all be reduced to economic value.

We may, for example, decide as a society to place a basic economic safety net under all citizens. We might say that all children have the right to food, dental and medical care, clothes, shelter, and education. If we do so, we have stepped beyond capitalism and made a political choice. Capitalism cannot guarantee such "goods."

Capitalism, then, offers a severely limited answer to the human question: How shall we organize the economic activities of our society? It cannot offer political, artistic, or religious advice because it has no way to measure their value.

But having said this, we must come back to the basic strength of capitalism. It produces more goods and services for more people than any of the alternatives.

There may be pockets of hunger in the United States, but famine has never been a problem here. Conversely, if you name the countries that have experienced famine during the last fifty years, you will in general name countries where the government has tried to "manage" the economy and failed.

Socialism has one overwhelming weakness: It undermines human energy and creativity. Societies that try to guide their economies end up with stagnant economies. After a half century, the Soviet Union lags far behind the United States in productivity. China has found it necessary to experiment with capitalist incentives.

In the New Testament, James pointed out that faith without works is worthless. A similar argument can be made here. The poor don't need rhetoric about justice. They need food. And food is more often available in a productive capitalist environment.

The socialist vision of an egalitarian society will always appeal to serious Christians, for it has much in common with the Old Testament prophets. Like the prophets, the socialist visionary cares about the poor. Unfortunately, socialists have not been able to implement their vision successfully in a fallen world. Evil is simply too pervasive.

Capitalists do not normally focus on the poor so directly. Not that Christian capitalists don't care about the poor; many of them do. But capitalists tend to be a practical lot. They accept the fact that our world is fallen, and so they implement the economic system that most often and most successfully cares for the poor.

## Forms of Capitalism

Pure laissez faire capitalism is not, in my opinion, a serious option for an evangelical Christian. Some business practices are legal, but immoral. A good salesman, for example, will often have an opportunity to make a sale that is not in his client's best interests. In extreme cases, to make such a sale would be oppression. The Old Testament prophets demanded social action and pointed out that God expects us to side with the oppressed. We need a government that takes an active role in protecting its citizens. And as individuals we need to be active in helping to formulate legislation that would protect consumers.[3]

Socially concerned evangelicals tend to lean toward welfare state capitalism, and that position is certainly a defensible one. However, welfare state capitalism is, in my opinion, unwise, because it depends upon relatively high tax rates. Evidence demonstrates conclusively that people in higher tax brackets tend to quit working when tax rates get too high. Society is better off with lower tax rates and citizens who work harder.

In the end, then, I find guided capitalism to be preferable for very practical reasons. This version of capitalism has the most potential for creating a society that can care for the poor.

# PART III
# AN ETHICAL SYNTHESIS

# 8

# Understanding the Biblical Vocabulary

I turned sixteen in the late 1950s, and like most teenagers, I loved cars. To this day, my heart skips a beat when I see a classic 1955 Ford Thunderbird; I'd love to own one! At the time, however, it never occurred to me to think seriously about buying myself a car. I worked, of course, but the money I earned was for college. Not until a few years ago was I able to allow myself the liberty and luxury of buying a new, sporty car I really liked. (Okay, I'll admit it: I had just turned forty. But there was more to it than that.)

For years I had heard sermons on materialism. I knew the commandment against coveting and the verses about the love of money being the root of all evil. Because I had been saturated with a religious perspective that emphasized self-denial I could not admit to myself how much I wanted certain things. I see now that I didn't understand what the Bible meant by greed or covetousness. Nor was my self-denial based on altruistic motives, for I certainly did not know that I was called to care for the poor, fight oppression, and practice justice.

Over the years I have studied what the Bible teaches about money and have moved closer, I believe, to a biblical position on the matter. Scripture teaches that the desire for and pursuit of material possessions is appropriate human behavior. However, that teaching is not immediately obvious.

The "thou shalt nots" of Scripture are in general far louder than the affirmations that balance them. In the Old Testament, the Ten Commandments forbade theft and murder in the strongest possible terms. In the New Testament, Jesus, in a quiet, winsome manner, taught that we should love one another. The voices are different, yet both reflect the same perspective.

This pattern in biblical teaching is particularly pronounced in passages dealing with wealth and poverty. Some of the more obvious passages forbid pursuing wealth in destructive ways, and there are strong injunctions against coveting and against oppressing the poor. Yet other passages teach that God has given us all things for our enjoyment, and that we are free to "want," that is, to desire to possess and enjoy the good things of this world. These perspectives are entirely compatible, but to see this clearly we need to look at this teaching first in its negative form.

### Greed

Greed is inordinate desire and Paul states that greed is idolatry (Eph. 5:3–5; Col. 3:5–6), and the spiritual leaders of the church (elders) are warned against this sin (1 Tim. 3:2–3). Luke records Jesus' warning against greed in the well-known parable about the rich farmer and his bulging barns (Luke 12:13–21). At the end of the parable, Jesus calls the farmer a fool and adds, "This is how it will be with anyone who stores up things for himself but is not rich toward God" (vs. 21). But look again at that conclusion. The rich fool is not condemned for his wealth but for the poverty of his relationship with God. Greed, in short, is putting the possession and enjoyment of material things before love of God. This is also a good definition of materialism.

It might be possible to distinguish between greed and materialism. Greed has to do with the excessive desire to acquire material goods, money, or whatever is of the most value in a given society. Materialism has more to do with one's overall philosophy of life: that is, a preoccupation with the material to the exclusion of the spiritual or intellectual; a belief that the only real value lies in material things. But at a fundamental level, they are the same. Both involve worshiping the creation rather than the Creator.

Matthew 6:19–21 is one of the most disturbing passages in the Bible having to do with wealth. There Jesus says, "Do not store up for yourselves treasures on earth" (vs. 19). How can we possibly deal with such a passage? What do we do with our pension plans; our policies insuring life, health, and cars; our savings accounts, and our money market funds? Did Jesus mean for us to take him seriously? Of course! Did he mean for us to take him literally? I think not. This passage must be interpreted in a full biblical context, and that includes both Old Testament passages that consider wealth a blessing and New Testament epistles that accept the presence of wealthy people in the church. Jesus forbids treating God's gifts as our greatest treasure.

After he encountered Jesus, Zacchaeus returned his ill-gotten gain and gave to the poor, but the context indicates that he was still wealthy. Jesus did not condemn him for that. Both Paul and James had specific words of advice for the rich in the church, but neither assumed that those people should divest themselves of their riches. The broader biblical perspective makes it absolutely clear that personal poverty is not an essential characteristic of the committed Christian. Freedom from greed and materialism is.

This perspective underlies Paul's advice to Timothy:

"Godliness with contentment is great gain. For we brought nothing into the world, and we can take nothing out of it" (1 Tim. 6:6–7). A few sentences later, Paul warns about those who have wandered from the faith because of their preoccupation with wealth. "The love of money is a root of *all kinds of* evil" (v. 10). Note, however, that he does not say that money itself is evil—it is *the love of* money that is evil. Wealth is not inherently evil; greed and materialism are. They make an idol of money.

Paul does not call the rich in the church to personal poverty, but he does call them to humility and a proper perspective on their wealth (1 Tim. 6:17–19). They must not trust in their wealth, but in God. Furthermore, as good stewards, they are to use their wealth for good deeds.

As I write these words, I have before me the business section of the *Los Angeles Daily News* that includes a column on youthful entrepreneurial chic. The piece tells of an eighteen-year-old real estate agent from Woodland Hills who was only twelve when he started dabbling in the silver market. He told the reporter, "My goals are really to make money. I know that sounds kind of dirty, but I'm here mainly to make money." Then there is the nineteen-year-old millionaire owner of a carpet and furniture cleaning company who began working when he was nine and now has ulcers and gray hair.[1]

While I admire the obvious ability of these young men—and certainly their business achievements are noteworthy—their personal philosophies make them close kin to the rich fool in Jesus' parable.

The desire for a new car or a large house is not evil. That desire can, however, lead one to compromise other commitments. And when it does that, it becomes evil.

Let's be specific. If the quality of my work is good enough, the commensurate wage value may allow me to enjoy good things. But when the demands of my business career or the desire to accumulate bigger and better things begin to undermine my relationship with my wife and children or my commitment to my local church, it may be time to back away from those demands. God intends us to work for a living and to enjoy the goodness of his creation as the fruit of that work. But when the desire to possess and enjoy God's creation eclipses our desire to live in relationship with God and with his people, that desire has become an evil for us.

## Covetousness

As a youth I tended to lump covetousness with greed and materialism. Clearly, however, they are quite different. Greed and materialism transform simple desire into idolatry. Covetousness is the excessive desire for a particular object belonging to another, which really amounts to a desire to take that object away from the person and have it for one's self.

Some years ago one of my teaching colleagues owned the very '55 Ford Thunderbird I had always wanted. This brought back all my old longings and youthful memories. Were those desires evil? Did I covet my colleague's car? Not really. My desire to own his car never brought me to the point where I would have been willing to manipulate him into a situation where I could take his car. But if it had—if my desire for his car had burned within me to the point where it even interfered with my ability to enjoy him as a person—then I would have gone beyond simple desire to covetousness.

Don't misunderstand. I am not equating lethargy with godliness. It was not that I didn't want the car enough to go after it. But my commitment to Christ led me to be committed to my relationship with my colleague. And because of my commitment to that relationship, it never even occurred to me to want to deprive him of his car.

This interpretation of covetousness provides a perspective for understanding much of the prophetic preaching about wealth and poverty. Ezekiel, for example, castigates the princes and officials for using their position to rob the people. The common people are likewise castigated for robbing the weak—widows, orphans, and aliens (Ezek. 22:23–31). Both wanted to possess some part of God's creation more than they wanted to live in relationship with God's people. Again, it is not the simple possession of wealth that is condemned, but the faulty relationship between an individual and wealth. When the desire for wealth eclipses the desire to live in right relationship with our neighbor, we are guilty of the sin of covetousness.

## Oppression

The logical outgrowth of covetousness is oppression. But the Old Testament shows particular concern with the oppression of the poor and with God's demand that they be treated justly, so we need to pay particular attention to this specialized case.

From the beginning, God recognized that the strong have great temptation to take advantage of the weak, and the Old Testament reflects this in specific ordinances and repeated warnings. The prophets regularly proclaimed God's special concern for the poor, and the law forbade the people of Israel to take interest payments from the poor (Lev. 25:35–38).

In their pre-capitalist culture, the Hebrew people had no way of investing surplus capital. Hence, no one could borrow to "get ahead." One borrowed money only to deal with a present need—to buy food, for example. For the rich to take interest under such circumstances would display callous lack of concern. The rich, therefore, were told to make interest-free loans to the poor. The poor, in turn, were responsible for returning the borrowed money. But returning the money was adequate; no interest was due.

From this specific command we can draw a general

principle: The strong are not to take advantage of their position to extract concessions from the weak. Jacob forced Esau to give up his birthright for food. It would be hard to imagine Esau treating his birthright with such disregard unless there were special circumstances not recounted in the text. We don't know the details, but we do know that Jacob saw an opportunity to use the situation to extract a commitment from Esau that he might not have given in other circumstances. That was oppression.

The prophets consistently and vehemently castigated the rich for using their economic position to manipulate the poor to their own advantage. Amos, for example, condemned the people of Israel because

> They sell the righteous for silver,
>> and the needy for a pair of sandals.
> They trample on the heads of the poor
>> as upon the dust of the ground
>> and deny justice to the oppressed (Amos 2:6–7).

Note, however, that Amos did not rail against wealth itself. Instead, he castigated the wealthy for using their power to deny justice to the poor.

The psalmist pictured God as the champion of the poor and oppressed.

> My whole being will exclaim,
>> "Who is like you, O LORD?
> You rescue the poor from those too strong for them,
>> the poor and needy from those who rob them"
>> (Psalm 35:10).

The prophetic stance is not against wealth but against bullies, not against those who *have* but against those who *take*. The godly, whether rich or poor, are to be like God himself; their daily conduct must embody justice because God is just.

## Justice

The Old Testament often uses the word *rich* as if it were synonymous with *oppressor* and *poor* as if it were synonymous with *oppressed*. And in Old Testament society that was often the case. Is it always so? Are the rich always the oppressors and the poor always the oppressed? No, of course not.[2]

The Old Testament writers, inspired by God, recognized that sloth brings poverty, as does evil-doing. Conversely, the Old Testament is full of good and just men who were wealthy (consider Abraham and Job). Furthermore, wealth was often promised as a blessing to those who lived in obedience to the law (Deut. 28:1–14). So the Old Testament perspective on wealth has two distinct, almost contradictory, strands.

Intellectually, I understand that fact. I understand that I am called to grasp the truth conveyed by each of those strands and to live in ways that reflect the full teaching of Scripture. Nonetheless, I find the simple presence of that first strand disconcerting whenever I read the Old Testament.

I admit to being affluent, perhaps even wealthy. Certainly most Third World Christians would see me that way. I go to the office each day where I keep the financial books for several rather ordinary businesses. I supervise two employees who help me with this task, and we work together in Christian harmony. At the end of the day I return home to my family. I do not believe that simply earning a decent salary makes me an oppressor. How, then, can I reconcile these strands?

Let's begin by recognizing the basic simplicity of the biblical commands. The Old Testament often formulates specific commands in the negative: "Thou shalt not. . . ." We are not to perform acts contrary to the nature of the God. We are not to destroy people, marriages, or reputations. We are not to act out of hatred. And we are not to deprive the poor of a secure place in society by depriving them of justice in the courts. Judges must not accept bribes (Exod. 23:6–8; Deut. 16:18–20). Government officials must not pass laws that conflict with God's Law: "Woe to those who make unjust laws" (Isa. 10:1). The context (vv. 1–4) indicates that this lament applies particularly to those who use unjust laws to oppress the poor and the widows. Business people must not defraud customers by using false weights (Lev. 19:35–36; Deut. 25:13–16). In sum, the Old Testament called the Hebrew people to just relationships in every area of their lives and their society.

In the Old Testament context, *justice* has a very narrow meaning. It is used in conjunction with laws, courts, and governmental officials. Hebrew law was broader than contemporary law. It included criminal law, civil law, and ethical injunction. But our differing concepts of law should not disguise the common element. Justice for both ancient Hebrew society and for our contemporary society is measured by an objective, commonly recognized standard.

*Just* is a legal term, not a synonym for *good* or *laudable*. Some Christians, however, have a tendency to use the words *just* or *unjust* where there is no clear agreed-on standard.[3] In recent years for example I have heard concerned Christians declare President Ronald Reagan "unjust" for cutting the budget for social services while expanding the military budget. Such proclamations mean little more than "I disapprove." Using the words *just* and *unjust* in this manner muddies the waters.

The unjust (or unrighteous) person is one who performs acts forbidden by the law—either direct transgressions, such as theft or adultry, against individuals, or indirect transgressions that deprive others of their political and economic rights.

Hosea and Micah both chastised business people for using dishonest scales (Hosea 12:7–9; Mic. 6:9–11). Amos condemned the more subtle sin of attitude in those who could hardly wait for the Sabbath to end so they could get

on with their money-making (Amos 8:4–6). Jeremiah
pronounced a woe on the people who wanted to build a
palace unjustly, requiring their countrymen to "work for
nothing, not paying them for their labor" (Jer. 22:13).
Such practices are oppression and extortion (Jer. 22:13–
14, 17).

Amos declared that God's judgment would come on
Israel because the powerful actively oppressed the poor.
"You oppress the righteous and take bribes and you
deprive the poor of justice in the courts" (Amos 5:12).
Micah charged that the unjust wanted to deprive others of
their fields, their land, their inheritances. The writer of
Ecclesiastes 5:8 bemoaned the fact that unjust governmen-
tal officials protected each other in such practices.

The just person, by contrast, has two broad characteristics: he doesn't do what the law forbids, and he does
what he should; namely, care for the poor and the
oppressed.

The first characteristic is most common. The just
man avoids doing what is forbidden by law: worship of
idols, adultery, robbery, and acts of "oppression" (Ezek.
18:5–9).

But God asks more of us than mere restraint; he
requires positive action. Therefore, the just person actively cares for the poor and the oppressed. "This is what the
Lord says: Do what is just and right. Rescue from the
hand of his oppressor the one who has been robbed. Do
no wrong or violence to the alien, the fatherless or the
widow, and do not shed innocent blood in this place" (Jer.
22:3). In another passage, Jeremiah praised the previous
king because "he defended the cause of the poor and
needy" (22:15–16). Zechariah reminded the people that
God had long ago commanded his people to see that
justice was done and to show kindness and mercy to each
other, particularly to the widows and the orphans (Zech.
7:8–10).

The rich gained power through their riches. They
had ample opportunity for dominating the poor. The rich

had the right, for example, to keep a pledge against a loan. But if the pledge was a cloak, the law required that it be returned at night so that the poor borrower would at least have its warmth while he slept. The rich of our society often complain of "cash flow" problems, but such problems are trivial compared to the problem of the destitute who live literally from hand to mouth. The rich, therefore, must be careful to pay wages daily where necessary, because the poor count on that wage for their very existence (Deut. 24:10–15).

Justice and injustice, then, are characteristics of individual actions. Just actions reflect the very character of God. Unjust actions are the reverse. This is true for both the average citizen and for government officials. The unjust actions of a king usually affect more people than do those of the common citizen, but they are still the unjust actions of an individual.[4]

## Summary

The scriptural teaching on greed, covetousness, and oppression does not suggest that the simple possession of wealth is wrong. Yet that position is widely held and taught. Where did such an idea come from?

Two possibilities come to mind. First, as we have noted, the Old Testament often uses the terms *poor* and *oppressed* synonymously. It likewise calls the *rich* the *oppressor*. An uncritical reading of the Old Testament concludes with the faulty generalization that all of the rich are oppressors.

The second source of this misunderstanding is the common tendency to make "category" mistakes. We apply the term unjust to a situation rather than to an action. Our economic system allows widely different levels of wealth and poverty to coexist, and we sometimes react emotionally with the cry, "That is not just or fair!" But poverty and wealth are not always the result of injustice. Poverty can be a symptom of a fallen world.

Poor widows are most often poor because of the untimely death of their husbands, not because of the harsh injustice of society. That fact in no way diminishes their need, but their poverty cannot be blamed on injustice. *Unjust* can only apply to actions and people, not to situations.

Wealth may be gained through hard work, intelligence, and creativity. Anyone who would charge such hard workers with injustice simply because they are rich in a world where some are still poor is likely guilty of greed and envy. As Paul admonished, "Who are you to judge someone else's servant? To his own master he stands or falls" (Rom. 14:4).

What, then, follows from all of this? First, we see that the Bible does not condemn the desire for worldly goods, but it does condemn perversions of that desire. Specifically, the Bible condemns desire that eclipses our love for God, our love for those around us, and our love for the weak and the poor. There are, therefore, limits on the pursuit of wealth. To transgress those limits is to be guilty of greed, covetousness, and oppression.

Second, God is not against wealth, but oppression. So Christians must reject any practice that supports oppression. Stated positively, Christians must reflect the very character of God. They must be known for their love of justice.

# 9

# The Rich and the Poor: Rights and Responsibilities

From one end of the Bible to the other rings out a curse on the rich. It is useless to try to get out of this by saying that it is talking about the wicked rich, or that this is the problem of another era. The prophetic and apostolic words are strikingly clear.

—Jacques Ellul
*Money and Power*: 137

A careful reading of the Bible will indicate that the rich are condemned only for the misuse of riches. . . . It is sometimes suggested that Amos, to take one example, demeaned riches in themselves. But this is not so.

—John White
*The Golden Cow*: 59

**C**learly I agree with White and those who see wealth as a blessing rather than the reward of sin. And yet Ellul has a point: the New Testament contains some very difficult passages on the subject of wealth and possessions. In fact, several explicit passages in the New Testament come close to condemning wealth and the wealthy directly: "Blessed are you who are poor" (Luke 6:20). "Woe to you who are rich" (Luke 6:24). "If you want to be perfect, go, sell your possessions and give to the poor, and you will have treasure in heaven" (Matt. 19:21).

It is just such passages that led Jim Wallis to state: "the New Testament condemns, not just improper attitudes toward wealth, but also the mere possession of undistributed wealth."[1] If he is correct, then the New Testament stands in fundamental conflict with the Old Testament. Is this so?

Ellul, for one, believes that it is. He admits that wealth is a blessing in the Old Testament but holds that it is condemned without qualification in the New Testament. In the end he despairs of finding a coherent interpretation. "We well know that these contradictions [in Scripture] are usually only apparent, for the unity of the spirit is powerfully revealed. But with wealth the situation is different."[2]

I disagree with this. And this is where the interpretive premises we discussed earlier become crucially important. If the same God stands behind both testaments, we must assume that there is a basic compatibility. Even though integrating the two may be difficult, we must assume it is possible.

## The Rights of the Rich

The presence of evil in this world often makes it necessary to speak the truth about God's creation in paradoxical assertions. Wealth is a perfect example. We must insist as strenuously as possible that wealth is a "good" while taking great care to warn the rich about its dangers. Only this paradoxical perspective makes sense out of the biblical data.

As we have seen, the Old Testament prophets never condemned wealth itself, yet condemned unmercifully those who oppressed others for the sake of wealth. The New Testament does exactly the same: It implicitly values wealth while clearly stating its dangers. Ellul may well be correct in holding money to be one of the fallen powers that would take us captive (one of the major themes of his book *Money and Power*). Nonetheless, wealth remains a blessing in the New Testament.

In the Sermon on the Mount, Jesus taught that wealth should never be treated as one's treasure (Matt. 6:19–21), and in another instance he pointed out that the rich can enter the kingdom of God about as easily as they can go through the eye of a needle (Mark 10:24–25). Note, however, that he did not say that members of the kingdom cannot be wealthy. He said that the rich will find it difficult to *enter* the kingdom of God—not that they cannot enter. The danger of wealth is that it tempts those who possess it to focus their lives on their money; they allow it to displace God himself. If they are to enter the kingdom of God, Jesus said, they must give up their idolatry; they must stop treating wealth as their ultimate treasure. Because the rich would find this to be difficult indeed, Jesus warned, they would therefore find it difficult to enter the kingdom.

Jesus also accepted the rich, those who believed in him, as his followers—like Zacchaeus and Joseph of Arimathea. When Zacchaeus, the dishonest tax collector, repented, he made reparation for his dishonest gains. He was not impoverished as a result, yet Jesus said that the kingdom had come to Zacchaeus's house. Nothing in the text indicates that Jesus condemned the man for retaining some of his possessions (Luke 19:1–10).

But while these passages allow for wealth, that is certainly not their focus. Most of them center on the great dangers of wealth and warn against storing up earthly treasures. Money holds great power over us and easily becomes an idol. Thus, we cannot escape the paradox that Jesus held wealth to be a good and yet warned about its power to corrupt.

The New Testament church exhibits this same paradoxical position. Ananias and Sapphira were condemned not for their wealth, but for their deceit (Acts 5:1–11). James condemned granting deference to the wealthy in the church, but not their presence there (James 2:1–13). Paul condemned the insensitivity of the wealthy in Corinth (1 Cor. 11:17–34). Some of them were literally feasting at the agape meal (love feast) in front of poorer brothers and sisters in Christ who went hungry! The apostle never objected to their wealth, nor did he suggest that they were responsible to divest themselves of it. But he did tell them they should eat at home rather than offend the poorer members of the congregation. In his letter to Timothy, Paul admonished the rich to be generous and not place their hope in their riches (1 Tim. 6:17–19). The leaders of the New Testament church knew the potential evil of money.

The conclusion is inescapable. The problem is not wealth, but an inappropriate attachment to or desire for wealth. The rich have a right to participate fully in the life of the church, and not to be condemned for their wealth. The church must not condemn either the rich or their money; it does, however, have a spiritual obligation to warn the wealthy of the dangers inherent in their wealth. Furthermore, the church must remind the wealthy of the rights of the poor.

## The Rights of the Poor

When I was a child, my parents often told me: "Rights and responsibilities go together. You cannot have the rights you want without shouldering the corresponding responsibilities." I have said the same thing to my own sons. "If you want the right to listen to your music, you are responsible to play it low enough that you do not disturb others." There is an element of truth in this, but like much homespun wisdom, it is a partial truth that cannot be applied in every situation.

The Hebrew prophets spoke out vigorously on behalf of the poor. And central to their message is the idea that the poor and needy have rights without corresponding responsibilities.

First, *the poor have the right to expect that the wealthy and the powerful will come to their defense even when this means that the wealthy and powerful must act against their own interests.*

Poverty saps people of material, emotional, and physical strength, often leaving them helpless. Since they cannot defend themselves when attacked, the strong must defend them. The best example of this can be seen in God's actions toward us; he models the behavior he expects of us. God defends the poor and the needy (Ps. 140:12) and commands us to do the same (Ps. 82:1–4).

The radicals of the 1960s and 1970s insisted that the poor had rights *in spite of their poverty,* and that society was responsible for creating structures that would protect those rights. During that period many conservative evangelical preachers and teachers began to acknowledge the truth of those radical assertions. They came to see that society's responsibility to protect the rights of the poor had always been clearly stated in the Bible. Christians simply had not seen it there before.

For example, the wealthy have always been able to afford legal counsel when necessary. If justice is to be served in the courts, such counsel must be available to rich and poor alike. This is possible only when those who *have* provide for those who *have not,* thus guaranteeing justice for all. There is a price tag attached to this, but it is a legitimate expense. Justice cannot be limited to those who can afford it.

Secondly, *the poor have the right to call on the wealthy and the powerful to create social structures that allow those at the very bottom of society to improve themselves.*

In the Old Testament culture, a bankrupt man could enter voluntary servitude, thus selling his future labor to pay his debts. But even in the poorest of circumstances—

the abject poverty of slavery—a Hebrew man retained some rights, and one of those was a legally established way out of slavery.

Thus the Hebrew slave retained hope. There were provisions in the law that would allow him to buy his freedom. But even where this was not possible, the slave had a second hope; the law promised him freedom at the end of seven years (Lev. 25:1–7; Deut. 15:1–15). Thus, in dire circumstances one could sell seven years of future labor; but after that, there was another chance!

The legal system in the United States distinguishes between a sale and a lease. A sale is a permanent transfer of ownership; a lease transfers the use of property for a specified term. The Hebrews had a similar system. Property (a house) within a walled city could be sold. But houses or land outside a walled city could not be sold; that property belonged to the Lord (Lev. 25:23–24, 29–31).

At the end of the conquest under Joshua, the land of Canaan was divided among the tribes—it was given to them for their perpetual use. A family that fell into poverty could sell the use of their land until the next Year of Jubilee. That is, they could lease it for up to forty-nine years, at which time it reverted back to them. But it could not be sold permanently. Thus, one generation of a family could not deprive the next generation of hope. In this way, God, through societal structures, provided a bulwark against a permanent underclass (Lev. 25: 10, 13, 17).

Another Hebrew law insured that the poor did not go without food. The law commanded landowners to leave the grain at the edges and corners of the fields for the poor. Furthermore, the fields were to be harvested only once. Whatever was missed on the first pass was to be left for the poor (Lev. 19:9–10; 23:22; Deut. 24:19–22). One of the most beautiful stories in the Bible, the story of Ruth and Boaz, illustrates this practice.

God demands nothing less than godlike behavior from the wealthy, and gives them responsibilities *for the poor* by virtue of their wealth. This godlike quality shows itself in their being a father to the fatherless and a defender of the widows (Ps. 68:5–6). Piety without concern for the needy is simply unacceptable (Isa. 58:1–10; Matt. 25:31–46; Eph. 4:28; James 2:14–17; 1 John 3:16–18).

We must add, however, that the wealthy also have rights. They have the right to justice in the courts, which are not to favor rich or poor (Exod. 23:1–2). Furthermore, the Bible prohibits theft and thereby validates the rights of ownership (Exod. 20:15) Stealing from the rich cannot be condoned in the name of social action.

In summary, the greater burden falls on the rich. The Bible does give them rights, but it focuses on their responsibility for the poor. The poor have the right to call the rich to that responsibility.

# 10

# Economic Perspectives on Justice and Oppression

There was once a man who hired two bricklayers to work for him. Before the work was completed, however, the man received an urgent call and had to leave on a short trip and was unable to settle on a wage with his two workers. He promised that as soon as he returned he would pay them justly. He asked that they complete the work and keep track of their time and labor. Since he was known in the community as an honest man who kept his word, the bricklayers did as he requested and completed the job.

On the man's return, the three agreed quickly on the total price to be paid for the job. Then the employer asked both bricklayers how the money should be split between them.

The first man, who had laid most of the bricks, suggested that the money be split according to their productivity. The second man felt this solution would be unjust. He acknowledged that the first man had more natural talent for bricklaying and so had laid more bricks. He noted, however, that they had both worked conscientiously the same number of hours. It was only fair, therefore, that the money be split evenly between them.

Advocates of laissez faire capitalism will have little trouble advising the man in the story: productivity should be rewarded. But can the Christian accept that answer? Are the market system and justice compatible? What is our responsibility to those with less natural ability? Must they forever go without or live with less? Shouldn't the two men receive equal payment?

But we must not forget that we live in an evil world. If we force the talented bricklayers of this world to share equally with those who are less talented and less productive, what incentive will they have for working at their full capacity? Won't they soon begin to wonder why they should work so hard when those who accomplish considerably less make the same amount?

These are tough but important questions. And to address them, we must look at three areas where Christians have often sensed injustice and oppression: wages, Third World development, and commodities prices.

As we do this, we must remember our finitude. We cannot, for example, eradicate hunger in Africa today. The Sahara Desert is moving south because of technological changes and misuse of the land. A solution, if we can find one, will be slow because it will demand cultural changes. In Ethiopia the problem is not technological or agricultural, but political. The leaders of that country do not want to eradicate hunger. They want to eradicate their opposition. In addition to these technological, cultural, and political constraints on what we can accomplish, there are also economic constraints, and these demand serious reflection. At this juncture, the focus of our analysis will not be theology or ethics, but economics. The key question is not "What *should* be done?" but "What *can* be done?"

## Wages

Labor economics is the first of those constraints, and to examine this we begin by looking at the function of wages in our economic system.[1]

First and foremost, wages measure and reward productivity. Some people are more productive than others and thus provide more economic value to their employers. Wages may be a crude and imprecise measure of productivity, but there is a clear link between the two. Wages reward that productivity.

Farmers are paid better in the United States than in most African countries for the simple reason that they produce more food. No moral judgment is implied here. In fact, American farmers probably do not work as hard as their counterparts in Africa. They don't have to because of the technology and machinery available to them. Wages paid to farmers come directly from the quantity of food delivered to the market. And because American farmers have better equipment and more fertilizer, they can produce more food. One may regret the fact that African laborers lack proper tools and materials, but our sympathy does not raise farm productivity in Africa. By allowing wages to be set by the tension between supply and demand, the market system recognizes the various levels of productivity.

Second, wages measure and reward risk taking. Jobs have varying levels of risk, and those who bear the greater risk deserve to be compensated for doing so. A window washer on a high-rise office building will usually be paid more than the janitor in a small one-story school. Salesmen who work for commissions risk long periods without income, but they often are compensated handsomely. By allowing wages to be set to reflect levels of risk, the market system can reward those who are willing to bear the risk.

Third, wages are only one form of payment. As a college professor, I was paid relatively low wages, but I received other compensations. Professors must meet with their classes and hold office hours; other than that, they have a great deal of autonomy in their use of time. That autonomy has value. Furthermore, the physical environment in which I worked was quite pleasant, and the pace was leisurely. The freedom to set my own hours, the pleasant surroundings, and the leisure were all part of my compensation. (I want to emphasize here that leisure *is* a form of compensation. Prior to the Industrial Revolution in England, most people spent virtually their entire lives working to survive. Today, most of us can live comfortably with a forty-hour-a-week job. Some people, however, choose to work more than forty hours in order to enjoy a higher material standard of living. They give up their leisure to do so.)

The business world where I now work offers higher wages than the educational world; however, the business world imposes greater risks. Colleges give tenure; corporations don't.

Compensation for work or productivity comes in the form of money, leisure time, status, autonomy, opportunity, and pleasant surroundings, to name just a few. By allowing monetary wages to respond to market forces, the market system can offer a variety of compensation packages.

Finally, wages function as a signal in the market system. In developed countries, some sectors of the economy pay better than others. Low wages in a sector signal that too many people have chosen that line of work. Higher wages advertise that more people are needed.

In some instances, whole countries have lower wages than other countries. Here the low wages are an invitation to investors. After World War II, low wages (hence, low production costs) and a stable government in Japan attracted manufacturing jobs from the United States. This movement caused problems in Detroit and other industrial areas of the West, but it built a strong democratic, capitalist economy in Japan. Today, wages in Korea and

Taiwan are lower than they are in Japan, and Japan is beginning to lose jobs to those countries.

There are Christian writers who deplore the fact that wages are low in Central America; they don't recognize that these low wages signal potential profits. Unfortunately, the American business community cannot take advantage of that opportunity because of the political instability of Central America. But if and when the political system in that area stabilizes, business will follow that profit potential, build strong economies, and in the process provide jobs and income to the people of Central America.

Wages perform a valuable function for the individual in a capitalist society. They allow each person to choose a job that fits his or her talents. Each can choose employment with a risk level suitable to that one's individual temperament, and each can choose a form of compensation he or she finds pleasing.

However, the role that wages play in the capitalist system should also raise serious questions for the Christian thinker.

(1) The level of compensation we achieve in our work life is closely related to the natural gifts and talents we have inherited. How should a just society deal with the fact that such ability is not distributed evenly? Do we need to go beyond the market system in some cases? Consider the following:

Some forms of mental illness are apparently transmitted genetically, leaving certain individuals incapable of coping with modern society—not because of sloth but because of disability. As people created in God's image, the mentally ill have great value, but they produce little of economic value. Our society should choose to take care of these individuals, but to do that we must go beyond the market system, which recognizes only goods and services in exchange for economic value rendered.

Musicians and athletes are often paid very well for using abilities they inherited. The market system simply accepts the fact that they possess these talents and that people are willing to pay well to watch them perform. In this case, we do well not to intervene. Society is not harmed by allowing the market to provide such high compensation, and intervention would limit individual freedom without contributing anything of value in return.

(2) The market system lacks a mechanism for compensating people who provide services that cannot be valued economically. For example, pastors and social workers who serve in the decaying areas of our cities provide a valuable service, but one that is incommensurate with measures of economic value. Yet they deserve adequate and fair compensation. How do we decide what their compensation should be? How do we measure such value?

These two questions leave me perplexed, but they do not erase the fact that allowing wages to be set by the market is an inherent part of a market system. The only alternative is to risk the inefficiencies of centralized planning. And so, we cannot prevent the market from paying the talented brick layers more nor rescue the less talented from the economic consequences of their plight.

## Third World Development

In recent years the growing disparity between rich and poor in Third World countries has prompted the socially concerned to assert that "we ought to do something." They demand, often in general terms, that we fight "for justice" and "against oppression." This kind of blanket charge is singularly unhelpful, however, for it fails to address the tremendous problems involved in trying to bring agrarian societies into the modern industrial world. The simple fact is that the market system lacks a mechanism for doing this without pain.

As Christians, we certainly ought to be concerned and ought to do something—if we can respond constructively. Yet we will be unable to help appropriately unless we take seriously the economics of development. Consider the pattern of development of a typical society.

At the beginning, Culture X consisted of peasant farmers. Some did better than others economically, but from the perspective of a Western or developed country, the disparity between the rich and the poor was small—in fact, they were all considered desperately poor.

Then, economic development began. Investors from a developed country entered the picture and built a manufacturing facility that provided new jobs and income for members of Culture X. Along with this, a Western exploration team discovered substantial natural resources in one area of the country. Thus, economic development began in Culture X.

During the transition from a peasant society into a developed industrial society, the disparity between rich and poor expanded substantially.[2] The first members of Culture X to get jobs in the industrial sector had money to spend on new consumer goods that previously had been unattainable. Also, the first Culture X farmers to adopt modern technology began to enjoy the wealth such technology produces. The wealth enjoyed by these individuals did not necessarily make those at the bottom of society poorer, but it made the disparity more glaring.

In certain cases, however, the success of some actually made the poor poorer. When a few individuals began farming with modern techniques, their growing productivity increased the quantity of food available and lowered food prices. Of course this was a wonderful benefit to the nonfarmers of Culture X. But the farmers who continued to use the old technology were gradually forced to quit farming. Without means of support, they migrated to the city in hopes of gaining employment there. Those who were successful, eventually entered the growing industrial sector. During the transition, however, they lived in utter squalor.

The industrial development continued, and Culture X eventually mastered modern technology and moved into the "first" world. At that point, there was once again relatively little disparity between the poor and the wealthy.

We, of course, would see a substantial difference between the two economic groups in Country X after development occurred. But this is really a matter of perspective. In the original peasant society of Culture X, there was a clear disparity between the poor and the wealthy. As outsiders, we would not have seen this clearly because the whole society would have appeared so impoverished to us. But the members of Culture X would certainly have seen the disparity. That same problem of perspective affects us when we look at our own country. To members of a peasant society, everyone in the United States appears to be fabulously wealthy. After all, virtually everyone owns a TV and a car, famine is unknown, infant mortality is low, and many people live on to their seventies and eighties. In a world-wide context, there is relatively little disparity between the rich and the poor in a developed society.

Our illustration above also highlights one of the major problems of development. During the transition period from an agrarian society to an industrial society, a country may experience great disparity between the rich and the poor. Some people will be employed in modern office buildings while others struggle for existence in the slums; rich mechanized farmers will grow prosperous while surrounded by peasants who are near starvation. The problem is this: it is impossible for an agrarian society with little capital to develop into a modern industrial society, which possesses and needs tremendous capital, without suffering great pain in the transition. And neither capitalists nor socialists have found an effective solution for alleviating this pain.

The market system, however, has this to be said for it: market societies make the transition more quickly and more smoothly than do societies that try to control the process. As we noted earlier, the process is proceeding more smoothly in the Ivory Coast than Ghana and in South Korea than North Korea.

We have a tendency to think that "someone ought to do something" even when the situation is difficult or impossible to manage or change. We often cry "oppression" when things don't get better.[3] Such responses do little for those in need. We do better to recognize that there are economic constraints in the development process. We may be able to help. But we cannot circumvent the pain of development.

## Commodities Prices

When the price of items such as coffee, tin, lumber, or sugar fluctuate wildly on world markets, Third World producer countries find it difficult if not impossible to plan the development of their economies. Again, many—including some evangelicals—have a strong sense that *someone* ought to do *something:* "speculators" ought to be forbidden from profiting at the expense of the needy; the government should step in and support prices.[4] Here again, however, we are not dealing with oppressors but with harsh economic realities.

The West is often accused of controlling commodity prices, but that is blatantly false.[5] (The last ten years should have conclusively proved that we cannot control oil prices.) As with all prices, commodities prices respond to supply and demand.

Theoretically, of course, every economist knows how to "dampen" such wild fluctuations. When the price of a commodity swings too low, a government agency should begin a steady buying program. This would keep the price from falling further. The demand created would be artificial, but it would effectively stabilize prices. Later when the commodity price goes too high, the agency should begin selling, again stabilizing the price. Long-range planning could be far more effective if this could be done and it would also be tremendously profitable!

This economic prescription means simply—buy low and sell high. Obviously, no one knows how to do that consistently. Therefore, those who are recommending government intervention are saying in effect that the government should support prices by buying when prices seem to be low and then absorb the loss if prices never go back up. Furthermore, since the government has no resources other than those that come from the people, this implicitly asks the people to support the price of the commodity they themselves produce. That will aid no one.

In this situation, there simply is no oppressor. Third World countries are not immune to the law of supply and demand. If the price of a commodity falls, it simply means that there is an oversupply of the commodity. We cannot change that law; we should not ignore it.

Injustice and oppression thrive in our fallen world, but the pain and suffering do not themselves necessarily point to an oppressor. People who stumble may be hurt because of the law of gravity. Likewise, both governments and individuals who ignore basic economic laws can inadvertently undermine their economic well-being. Socially concerned Christians must recognize the existence of such laws and understand the constraints they place on us before they make value judgments about justice and oppression.

# 11

# The Ethics of Affluence

In the early stages of the Ethiopian famine, a friend of mine went to that country on a fact-finding trip for a Christian relief agency. He returned the day before Thanksgiving. On Thanksgiving Day, over a sumptuous dinner, we discussed the famine, and ended up asking ourselves, "How can we do this? How can we feast, knowing that people are dying of starvation in Ethiopia at this very moment?"

Our spirit cries out, "This should not be!" and, "There must be an answer!" But the simple truth is this: There is no answer—today. Perhaps we can rid the world of hunger within the next generation, but not today.[1] This is a fact, and we cannot begin to act responsibly until we face our finitude.

Our knowledge is limited. Some of our most fundamental religious questions seem to have no clear answers. God created us to live in fellowship with himself and to exercise dominion over his world. He provided the fruits of this world for us to enjoy, yet he calls us to put aside our right to enjoy the good fruits of his creation in order to help others in need. He calls us to proclaim the gospel to those who need to be reconciled with God, but this conflicts with his original mandate. The presence of evil in our world presents us with unresolvable dilemmas. We can spend a weekend relaxing by the lake or in helping in the inner city, but we cannot do both at the same time. What shall we do? How do we reconcile our conflicting responsibilities? Or can we reconcile them?

We were not created to deal with evil, and yet that is now our task as Christians. Until God reconciles all things to himself, we will live in an evil, divided world, and the presence of evil in our world renders us incapable of solving such dilemmas. At best, we will be able to divide our time between conflicting demands of an appropriate way under the guidance of the Holy Spirit. But we will never be able to generalize—to say, "This is how all Christians ought to divide their time."

Questions about social policy are equally baffling. There are families living in real need in every major city in the United States, but it is not clear how society can meet their need. During the sixties and seventies we tried providing money, but only succeeded in undermining family structures in the black community. At this junction if we cut back on welfare provisions, some people in real need will go without. If, on the other hand, we continue to provide, we risk exacerbating the problem. We also face the matter of the multitude of homeless living on the streets of our cities. Many of these men and women are mentally ill. Do we leave them uncared for, or do we risk taking away their civil liberties in order to force care on them? Again, there are no definitive solutions. Our knowledge is too limited.

Furthermore, our power is limited. We know how to grow enough food to feed the world and we know how to create a distribution system capable of providing food for everyone in the world, but we do not have the capacity to do it at this time. The task totally transcends our current resources.

In short, we must begin our ethical reflections by confessing our limitations. Modesty becomes God's creatures.

So we have come full circle—back to Kent Hartford's dilemma in chapter 1. And as we conclude, I want to describe briefly how I personally resolve some of the issues that have flowed through this book. Obviously I don't consider my conclusions definitive—how could they be in light of the previous few paragraphs! They are simply the way I personally resolve some of the conflicting demands in our affluent but fallen world. Perhaps they will be helpful to you as you grapple with these ethical issues.

## The Ethics of Competition

When my boys were small, they used to run foot races with each other. Once, after losing a race, one of the younger boys asked, "Did I win too?" Of course, he had not. Where there are winners, there must be losers. Most of us can accept this—in sports. But can we accept a world in which there are economic losers?

The Bible seems to be neutral on the subject of competition. Frankly, I cannot picture a *perfect* world in which competition still plays a role. It seems to me that in a perfect world we would play at sports for the sheer joy of play; we would work for the experience of creating and producing. But we don't live in such a world. Evil has altered the way we relate to each other, and this includes our economic relationships.

Capitalism is founded on the human propensity to compete for wealth and possessions. As in a foot race, where there are winners there must be losers. Yet unlike competition in sports, competition for wealth leaves most of us uneasy. Why? How should we evaluate the competition for wealth?

I would suggest that economic competition, much like human government, is a necessary part of life in a fallen world. As we have seen, wealth can be created on a global and national level. We do not live in a zero sum world. But as individuals we must often work in a zero sum context. If I make the sale, my competitor misses a sale. This competition for wealth contributes to our well-being in two very important respects: first, since most of us are lazy (at least some of the time), we need incentives to keep us working to capacity; and second, competition guarantees that those who use resources ineptly or irresponsibly will eventually be relieved of their responsibilities.

Thus, my defense of capitalism is both theological and pragmatic. Capitalism, by fragmenting power, keeps evil in check. It also, in my opinion, cares for the poor more effectively than alternative systems. While capitalism is *not* fundamentally Christian, it is the best economic system created thus far. It does, however, have weaknesses. I consider its encouragement of competition to be one of them.

Economic competition can crush the weak, and Christians are responsible to care for the weak. There are, therefore, times when the strong must refrain from using their strength out of concern for the weak.

In an earlier chapter I referred to Steinbeck's book *The Grapes of Wrath*. In that context I intentionally omitted an important part of the story: Migrant workers were streaming to California because the owners were advertising for farm laborers. Dust bowl farmers who had lost their farms had no way of knowing that California already had a glut of unskilled labor. They had no way of knowing that they would be pawns in a labor dispute. By advertising nationally, the owners were competing for workers in a market economy, but they were competing unfairly. Their strength oppressed the poor.

Some people lack the natural abilities to compete effectively. Others, because of their unique experiences, have lost the psychological ability to compete at all. It is not clear how we should care for such people. The

Christian must depend on the sensitivity and wisdom that comes from the Holy Spirit in making such decisions.

But such comments are qualifications. In general, competition seems to be a necessary and even a beneficial ingredient of economic life in a fallen world.

## The Ethics of Compensation

I work in management and am thus involved in settling wage levels. As a Christian, I am responsible to relate to other employees in ways that reflect the love and care of Christ. This means that I must see that the company pays its employees what it agreed to pay. That much is clear from the teachings of the prophets and the New Testament and needs no further comment. But what is my responsibility when I set wages and salaries? Should I merely pay what the market demands? Or must I raise the question of a "just wage"?

As we have discussed, the concept of justice always references an external, publicly recognized, and accessible standard. In demanding justice, the prophets did not appeal to their own internal sense of justice, but to the written law. However, there is no clear external standard for setting a just wage. The going wage in the market-place is external and accessible, but it is certainly not a standard of justice. It is merely the going rate at which employers and employees agree together to maintain an employment relationship.

The Bible, on the other hand, which is our authority as believers, does not address this issue. Nowhere does it speak of paying a just wage. Rather, the Scriptures remind unscrupulous employers that they must not withhold pay from workers once they have entered into an agreement. Thus, the phrase "a just wage" lacks clear meaning—both in the United States where wages are relatively high and in Third World countries where they are not.

The alternative to searching for an elusive "just wage" is simply to pay the market wage. Is this an adequate Christian response? In general, I believe it is. That conclusion is in fact a corollary to the position I took regarding competition. The market, via a competitive wage system, will in general allocate human resources more appropriately than will any alternative system.

My position, however, reflects my American context where poverty, while it exists, is relatively rare. Less than a fifth of our population experiences real need, and death by starvation has been virtually eliminated in our country. In a Third World context, a different answer might be appropriate.

Jesus told a parable about an employer who hired laborers to begin working at several different times in one particular day. At the end of the day, he chose to pay all of them exactly the same amount, whether they had begun working early in the morning or later in the afternoon. The employer knew that the wage of a day laborer would just barely cover food for the laborer's family. If he had paid them according to the hours they had worked, some families might have gone hungry that night. The parable draws attention to the fact that God is not only just, but also generous and merciful and that we are responsible to reflect those aspects of his character.

Christians who own and operate their own businesses have the freedom to pay more than a market wage, an action that may demonstrate compassion and concern. But while a decision to pay more than the market demands may be good, it is not more just. No external standard demands such behavior.

The question is: Should a Christian employer pay more than the market wage out of compassion and concern in a situation where the market wage will leave willing workers with less than a living wage? Perhaps so. Certainly the decision to do so would have biblical precedent. But a general answer is not possible. Such wages would be a gift from the employer to the employee, and one would need to know the specific situation in order to evaluate the wisdom of such a gift. So the question of compassion moves us from the ethics of compensation into the ethics of consumption and giving.

## The Ethics of Consumption

Most of us do not have large amounts of money at our disposal at one particular time. But over our lifetime, each of us will earn and spend a substantial sum. The earnings of the average U.S. family will exceed $1,000,000 ($25,000 per year for 40 years). Each of us will have some part in deciding how those dollars will be spent. We can choose to spend them on goods and services that we or our family will consume, or we can choose to give them away. We will decide a dollar at a time. And thus we are again back to the problem that introduced this book: Every time I choose to spend a dollar on myself, I am also choosing not to give that dollar to someone else. Since I live in an affluent society in a world where hunger still exists, those choices are difficult.

Some evangelicals respond to the tension between consumption and giving by condemning materialism. This response, however, lacks focus. A blanket condemnation gives us no guidance about how to decide such things as: How much should we save for retirement? How much should I consume beyond simple subsistence? In short, condemning materialism may sound noble—it may even make us feel better for a while—but it really doesn't mean anything.

Other evangelicals call us to a simple life-style, but this too is an inadequate response—and it lacks a clear biblical base. A simple life-style is not inherently more just, nor has it been shown to offer any real long-term aid to the poor. Whereas the above reaction lacks focus, this reaction focuses at the wrong point.

We are called to serve Christ and our neighbors, not to live a simple life-style. In some cases, of course, a life of service demands a simple life-style. One could not serve well in the ghetto and drive a Mercedes. But Christ calls us to himself and to his service, not to a particular life-style.

Several Christian writers have suggested a "theology of enough."[2] This idea holds promise, but it needs careful definition. When I say to myself, "You've had enough now," I am usually thinking about my weight. Used in that sense, the word *enough* has a negative connotation; it's a restriction. When a theology of enough suggests that I ought to limit my consumption because others do not have enough, it is advocating the simple life-style. Again, I must insist that such a perspective misrepresents the God of the Scriptures.

However, a theology of enough can also be a positive statement. When I see someone laboring at a task with inadequate tools, I might say, "You don't have good-enough tools for your job. You ought to buy better ones." Here, *enough* means *adequate* or perhaps *appropriate* and is related to a goal or a task. Used this way, a theology of enough may make a positive contribution to our thinking, suggesting that we ought to consume whatever is necessary to carry out the tasks God has given us.

For example, working in the American business world, I must dress appropriately for my position. When I worked at a commercial bank some years ago, I was expected to wear a suit. A sport jacket was not acceptable. A positive theology of enough would say, "Don't feel guilty about spending enough money on good clothes. They are necessary to your job." Suits, of course, come in a wide range of qualities. I chose to purchase suits that were "good enough" to do the job. They did not draw attention to themselves either as excessively expensive or as excessively cheap.

Then, when we have spent "enough" on ourselves, when we have spent appropriately, we should use some of the remainder to feast and celebrate in thanksgiving for God's goodness and we should give to others joyfully out of our abundance. Celebrating and feasting have clear biblical precedents; such celebrations were a key part of worship in both testaments. And giving to others is a natural expression of thanksgiving for God's goodness to us.

Even a *positive* theology of enough does not provide clear direction, of course. I don't ever know *definitively* how much is enough for the tasks God has given me, nor can I see a clear boundary between celebrating and indulgence. But personally I find this perspective very helpful. Christians, like everyone else in this world, must live with ambiguity, but such a positively formulated theology of enough provides some guidance in the midst of this.

## The Ethics of Giving

After consuming enough to do the tasks God requires of us, we are free to give. But giving can be destructive to the very ones it is meant to help. For example, an inheritance—a gift to the heirs—can destroy the recipients. The conflict generated by a will can cause bitter feelings, even make lifelong enemies within a family. Or, the inheritance itself can rot the moral fiber of the recipients.

There is substantial evidence that the American welfare system has helped to undermine the family structures of the poor. Massive gifts of grain to poverty-stricken countries have in some cases undermined the price structure in those countries and forced farmers to abandon the land and their work. In each of these cases the recipients were worse off after receiving the gift.

Nonetheless giving is both a natural inclination and an obligation. As indicated above, giving is the flip side of consuming. Logically we must eventually dispose of every dollar we receive, either by purchasing something that can be consumed, by giving it away, or by leaving it to our heirs at our death. When we know how much is enough for carrying out the tasks God has given us to perform, we will know both how much to consume and how much we are to give. This leaves two questions: "To whom shall we give?" and, "How shall we give?"

It seems appropriate to give an inheritance to one's children, and Scripture seems to assume this natural inclination. Many Americans today are able to leave a substantial bequest to their children, but parents must take care that their last gift is not destructive. The concept of enough may again be helpful. For example, the gift of a college education for one's grandchildren may enable them to become more involved in the work of the kingdom of God. A substantial inheritance may be appropriate to a child with good business sense and a commitment to furthering the Lord's work in this world. However, parents need not assume that all of their wealth should be passed to their children and grandchildren. Rather, they can ask, "What do my children need to carry out the tasks God has given them?" Parents can leave them enough for these tasks and give the balance to a ministry or work of God.

In discussing the ethics of compensation, I asked, "Should a Christian employer pay more than the market wage?" In short, should a Christian employer give to his employees beyond what they have earned? Unfortunately, most well-intentioned attempts to go beyond the market system do more harm than good, and paying more than the market wage may well be a case in point. In our culture, alternative ways of giving may be more appropriate—ways that build for the future.

An employer could, for example, create scholarships for the children of his employees, thus investing directly in human development. Several Christian organizations make loans to potential entrepreneurs in Third World countries who need help getting started. Such loans encourage economic development and productivity. Neither of these suggestions relate directly to the work of the church, but they value that which is fundamentally consistent with the work of the kingdom. Such gifts build people.

Some evangelicals condemn direct social action. I am not advocating that position. But I do believe that, in the long run, a healthy church contributes more to the physical well-being of people than does immediate aid. Personally, I give most often to missions and I would commend this to you. Some of my giving goes directly to people who are doing work God has laid on my heart. At other times, I try to give in ways that will build the superstructure of a strong church. I have given, for example, to seminary libraries in Third World countries and to organizations that translate and distribute Scripture. I believe such direct support for translations and theological education will strengthen the church and lead over time to more stable families and to a stronger economy. Thus, such a gift is both a gift to the church and a gift to the poor.

In the end, then, I do not believe that we need to agonize over our affluence. To the contrary, it should lead us to thanksgiving. It is a by-product of our healthy economic system and our stable society. We must, however, keep it in perspective. It is a gift from God. Like all gifts, it can be abused. And if abused, it can cause pain and suffering. Our focus must remain on God, not on his gift, if we are to enjoy it as he intended.

"Everything God created is good, and nothing is to be rejected if it is received with thanksgiving, because it is consecrated by the word of God and prayer" (1 Tim. 4:4–5). Nonetheless, we must "seek first his kingdom" (Matt. 6:33). God insists that we have no other gods before him (Deut. 5:7–8). And that prohibition includes the inordinate pursuit of affluence.

# Appendix
## A Critique of Three Alternative Perspectives

### The Ascetics

Ron Sider's book *Rich Christians in an Age of Hunger* has been one of the most influential books on the issue of Christian responsibility and world hunger. It makes a strong biblical case for concern for the poor and oppressed. However, while it is powerful, it is a one-sided statement that represents the ascetic tendency in contemporary evangelicalism.[1]

1. Sider notes that in the Old Testament wealth is often associated with oppression.

> God does not have class enemies. But he hates and punishes injustice and neglect of the poor. And the rich, if we accept the repeated warnings of Scripture, are frequently guilty of both.[2]

True, in the Old Testament "the wealthy" are almost synonymous with "the oppressors." But that is only part of the biblical message. There is a second major theme that balances this first theme: the Bible promises wealth to the faithful participant in the Old Testament covenant.[3] Sider neglects this second biblical theme, and to that extent, he misrepresents the Old Testament message.

2. Like all of us, Sider is influenced by his own perception and definitions, some of which may be unconscious and unacknowledged. In this case, it seems to me that Sider understands all human relations as "face to face" relationships. Take, for example, the Good Samaritan. The priest and the Levite were indeed at fault for ignoring the stranger, and the Samaritan was justly praised for going to his rescue (Luke 10:25–37). But it may be inappropriate to generalize that image beyond personal relationships. Sider quotes from 1 John 3:17–18, which calls on Christians to care for their brothers in need, and concludes:

> Again the words are plain. What do they mean for Western Christians who demand increasing affluence each year while Christians in the Third World suffer from malnutrition, deformed bodies and brains— even starvation? The text clearly says that if we fail to aid the needy, we do not have God's love—no matter what we may say. It is deeds that count, not pious phrases and saintly speeches.[4]

Sider's charge is unfair and seems to be designed to produce unjustified guilt feelings. I usually know what to do when I am confronted with immediate and short-term needs. I am not always sure how to deal with long-term needs and problems, or problems that occur outside my immediate environment. For example, how should the church minister to a schizophrenic who will not allow himself to be institutionalized but who clearly needs care? What is the proper response to massive needs such as Biafra in the 1970s or Ethiopia in the 1980s? Invoking "face to face" ethics simply does not provide meaningful guidance.

3. Sider also fails to deal with the ethical status of "equality." Is absolute equality a biblical commandment?

Sider seems to think not. Only great economic inequality is wrong.[5] Yet he sometimes rails against any differential.[6] It appears that Sider's heart cries out for equality while his mind recognizes that it is probably impossible and that it might not even be a biblical good.

These three points note how Sider's interpretation of Scripture affect his theology. The following points note assumptions Sider brings to the text from our culture that distort his understanding.

4. Sider focuses almost exclusively on the economics of distribution, on dividing wealth in general and food in particular, rather than on the economics of producing wealth.

> While Sebastian and Maria's twins lay dying, there was an abundance of food in the world. But it was not divided fairly. . . . It is because of this high level of meat consumption that the rich minority of the world devours such an unequal share of the world's available food.[7]

Sider never addresses the question: Is it immoral to consume the goods (food in particular) one produces?

The United States produces enormous amounts of food and could produce even more. The Soviet Union in contrast continually falls short of its food production goals. Does the Russian determination to maintain ineffective centralized control over its food production system place the United States under obligation to share its food with the Russian people? The people of the United States do in fact consume "more than their share of the world's food." They also produce more than their share. Dividing resources may be appropriate in some contexts. But it would seem that Sider's focus on "dividing resources" and "just distribution" has led him to ask the wrong question.

5. Sider never examines the effect of charity on the recipient. He calls for low-interest or no-interest loans for the poor, but neglects to mention the evidence that

suggests that such loans only encourage waste. We do not tend to value things we do not pay for.[8]

6. Sider confuses biblical life-styles with simple life-styles. He suggests, for example, that we take up gardening.[9] Gardening may indeed be a good hobby, and there are good reasons for valuing it. But a highly paid executive will be doing no one a favor by working less at his profession in order to follow a simple agrarian life-style.

7. Finally, Sider has not faced his own finitude and impotence. He acknowledges that prosperity is good, but argues that Christians "must lower their standard of living . . . because others are starving."[10] Yet he never suggests that such deprivation will help anyone. Apparently it does little but help Sider deal with his own uncomfortable conscience—and those are poor grounds for such a broad generalization.

Having said all of this, one must recognize Sider's tremendous compassion. A billion people in our world today have less than adequate food, and he is right to mourn their suffering. But his compassion seems to have left him without joy. He disclaims asceticism, yet that is clearly the tone of his book.[11]

## The Prosperity Preachers

The polar extreme can be seen in a group of writers and preachers who focus on prosperity to the virtual exclusion of legitimate concern for the poor. These folks assert—without apparent qualification—that God wants, intends, and promises wealth and prosperity for every Christian.[12] According to their teachings, the Bible promises wealth to every Christian on two conditions: that we stay out of debt and give liberally to God's work. One must only begin following these biblical injunctions in order to begin receiving God's promise of wealth. It is impossible to outgive God. Such teachers err in three ways:

1. They come very close to turning the teachings of the Bible into magic. In his classic study *Magic, Science and Religion,* Bronislaw Malinowski showed that magic and science are closely related.[13] Both offer a prescription for controlling the physical environment. Scientists vigorously repudiate magic, yet they have the same goals as magicians: both want to control. Religion, in contrast, does not seek control over nature but rather a relationship with its Creator. In this broad sense, then, Christianity is a classic religion. Its uniqueness is its claim that God has taken the initiative in establishing this relationship through Jesus Christ.

True magic tries to control impersonal forces to bring about personal ends, such as good crops, fertility, or revenge on an enemy. The wealth and prosperity teachers are of course concerned with receiving a blessing that they claim a personal God has promised to us. To this extent, their claims are utterly different from those of the animistic shaman. The wealth and prosperity teachers clearly understand that they are dealing with the personal God of the Bible. Nonetheless, there are striking similarities. "True prosperity is the ability to use God's power to meet the needs of mankind in any realm of life."[14] Meeting the needs of mankind is of course laudable, but I am uncomfortable with the phrase, "the ability to use God's power." That smacks of magic. In this way, their focus gives them much in common with more primitive forms of religion.

In short, they have lost the central focus of the Bible. Christianity is not about prosperity; it is about a personal relationship with God through Jesus Christ.

2. Wealth and prosperity teachers are naive interpreters of the Bible. Specifically, they treat the Bible as a collection of unrelated proof texts. For example, Gloria Copeland quotes Romans 13:8 to show that Christians should not be in debt.[15] She never mentions the context, which has nothing to do with economic issues. Rather, it is Paul encouraging Christians to fulfill their duties to

government. Or consider Elbert Willis's quoting of Mark 10:29–30 as God's guarantee that Christians will receive back in this life a hundred times what they give up for the sake of the gospel.[16] Yet Willis gives no indication that he might be dealing with a hyperbole.

3. Prosperity preachers often teach a "name-it and claim-it" approach to prayer. They assert that IF the Bible promises something, and IF a Christian prays in faith, then God WILL provide—without qualification. And that promise applies to wealth and prosperity.[17]

While many passages of Scripture do promise that Christians can have whatever they want through prayer, the fact that there are still hungry Christians in the world shows that there must be some qualifications. I do not disagree with the statement that God wants prosperity for us all. I would merely assert that there are some qualifications.

Wealth and prosperity teachers have recovered the idea that God wants to give good things to his children, but they have lost Sider's compassion.

## Institute for Christian Economics

David Chilton's *Productive Christians in an Age of Guilt Manipulators* is probably the best presentation of the Institute for Christian Economics. Advocates of this position seem to have a better grasp of modern economic theory than those who hold to the previous two positions. For example:

> "Investment" means *putting capital to work*. It aims at increased productivity, and thereby benefits *all*, not just the investor. *A true investment, meaning a non-fraudulent investment, in fact, cannot benefit the investor without benefitting others.*[18]

But advocates of this position bring inappropriate assumptions to the interpretive task.

1. This position confuses prescriptive law with descriptive law. If I say, "You ought to do thus and so," I am prescribing proper behavior. The Bible is full of such prescriptive laws. We *should not* use dishonest weights, for example.

If I say to my child, "If you lean over the rail too far, you will fall," I am describing how the law of gravity works. All scientific laws—and that includes economic laws—are descriptive. Descriptive laws are merely human attempts to describe how the universe works. They are at best approximations. Some laws are so inflexible—the law of gravity is a good example—that we treat them as unchanging. They are, nonetheless, still descriptions.

Chilton asserts that biblical laws when taken together entail the "law of supply and demand" which "is God's law, not subject to human control."[19] He also claims that any attempt to tamper with the capitalistic system amounts to rescinding God's law.

Now it is obviously true that we humans cannot change the way the physical universe operates nor rescind its laws. However, neither the law of supply and demand nor the capitalistic system deserves the status Chilton gives them. Claiming that the law of supply and demand is one of God's law shows little understanding of the status of laws in the philosophy of science.[20] He does not see that all description law is tentative. By imposing this misunderstanding on the interpretive process, he virtually guarantees that we will draw some false conclusions.

2. Chilton asserts, without any biblical support whatsoever, that we must not go beyond biblical legislation. To do so is legalism.[21] Taken literally, such a position is nonsense. (To cite just one example, we obviously need laws to govern automobile traffic.) However, Chilton makes the statement in the context of laws that prohibit discrimination, and he probably does not intend such a thorough application. His point seems to be that while discrimination is unethical, governments should not impose ethical standards on society other than

those mandated in the Old Testament. But even this milder application makes little sense. The Bible prohibits theft. In modern society, we must have legislation that can interpret the concept of theft into a complex business environment, and such law would certainly go beyond biblical legislation.

The tone of Chilton's book is beneath what we should expect from a writer attempting to respond to other Christian writers. Nonetheless, he is worth reading. He shows a better understanding of economic theory than other writers we have examined so far.

But in the end, Chilton's odd interpretive approach mars his argument so much that his economic point of view is lost.

# NOTES

## CHAPTER 1. FACING THE DILEMMA

[1] The introductory scene is freely adapted from a case study entitled "Rigor and Responsibility" by Robert L. Stivers (Case Study Institute, 1980. Distributed by the Intercollegiate Case Clearing House, Soldiers Field, Boston, Mass. 02163).

[2] See *World Development Report, 1983*(New York: Oxford University Press), Table I, 148–49. The per capita income for 80 percent of the countries of the world—including China and India—was below $5,000.

[3] See Roger Cohen, "All Latins Should Try Chile's Homemade Growth Recipe" *Wall Street Journal,*Sept. 30, 1988, 23. Cohen commends Chile's government for its economic management without approving Pinochet's authoritarian regime.

[4] Bonganjola Goba, "Contextual Understanding: The Problem in S.A. of Differing Perceptions and Analyses," *Transformation* 3:2 (April/June 1986): 18.

## CHAPTER 2. BIBLICAL INTERPRETATION

[1] For further information on contextualization, see the works by Bruce Nicholls and Charles Kraft in the bibliography.

[2] Ronald J. Sider, *Rich Christians in an Age of Hunger* (Downers Grove, Ill.: InterVarsity Press, 1984), 80–82.

## CHAPTER 5. ORIGINS OF WEALTH AND PROSPERITY

[1] Andrew J. Kirk, *New World Coming* (London: Hodder and Stoughton, 1984), 71.

[2] Jim Wallis, *Agenda for Biblical People* (New York: Harper and Row, 1976), 92.

[3] Tom Sine, *The Mustard Seed Conspiracy* (Waco, Tex.: Word Books, 1981), 26.

[4] Michael Novak, "Democratic Capitalism," *Transformation* 2:1 (January/March 1985): 18.

[5] Adam Smith, *The Wealth of Nations,* 5, quoted in Robert B. Ekelund and Robert F. Hebert, *A History of Economic History and Method* (New York: McGraw-Hill, 1983), 101.

[6] Ekelund and Hebert, *History,* 102.

[7] Paul Johnson, "Movement in the Market," *On Freedom* (Greenwich, Conn.: Devin-Adair, 1984), 42–43.

[8] Ibid.

[9] Michael Novak, *The Spirit of Democratic Capitalism* (New York: Simon and Schuster, 1982), 302.

[10] P. T. Bauer, *Dissent on Development* (Cambridge: Harvard University Press, 1981), 41, 97–98.

[11] Novak, *Spirit,* 234, quoting Reinhold Niebuhr, *Our Moral and Spiritual Resources for International Cooperation* (New York: The U.S. National Commission for UNESCO, 1956), 34.

[12] Novak, *Spirit,* 304. See also, David Morawetz, *Twenty-five Years of Economic Development: 1950 to 1975* (Baltimore: The Johns Hopkins University Press, 1977), 61.

[13] *World Development Report, 1983* (New York: Oxford University Press), 173.

[14] Bauer, *Dissent,* 76.

[15] Novak, *Spirit,* 300.

[16] P. T. Bauer, *Equality: The Third World and Economic Delusion* (Cambridge: Harvard University Press, 1981), 75. Also, Bauer, *Dissent,* 148.

[17] Richard M. DeVos with Charles Paul Conn, *Believe!* (Old Tappan, N.J.: Fleming H. Revell, 1975), 81. DeVos turns the argument on its head by marveling that 6 percent of the world's population have the ability to produce 45 percent of the world's automobiles, 60 percent of the world's telephones, and 80 percent of the world's televisions.

[18] Arthur Simon, *Bread for the World* (Paulist Press and William B. Eerdmans, 1975), 9.

## CHAPTER 6. ALTERNATIVE ECONOMIC SYSTEMS: AN INTRODUCTION

[1] Critics of capitalism often point to Central America to show that wealth does not "trickle down" to the poor in capitalist countries. But as Novak points out in *Will It Liberate?* (New York: Paulist Press, 1986), these countries have never really tried capitalism. They are effectively preindustrial and precapitalist in structure.

[2] See Robert G. Clouse, ed., *Wealth and Poverty: Four Views* (Downers Grove, Ill.: InterVarsity Press, 1984). Gary North, the most conservative of the authors, argues that the Bible teaches capitalism. John Gladwin argues for Christian socialism.

[3] The following books provide a good introduction to the market system. Bauer, *Dissent on Development* (Cambridge: Harvard University Press, 1981); Milton and Rose Friedman, *Free to Choose: A Personal Statement* (New York: Avon Books, 1980); George Gilder, *Wealth and Poverty* (New York: Bantam Books, 1981); Novak, *The Spirit of Democratic Capitalism* (New York: Simon and Schuster, 1982). Richard H. Leftwich provides a basic introduction to the theory of prices in *The Price System and Resource Allocation* (Hinsdale, Ill.: Dryden Press, 1979).

[4] Johnson, "Movement in the Market," *On Freedom* (Greenwich, Conn.: Devin-Adair, 1984), 43–44. Johnson offers an explanation of the fact that the United States is more efficient than Russia. "One can provide many explanations, but they all amount to the same thing. Economic efficiency is the consequence of making the right decisions. And making decisions correctly depends on access to accurate knowledge. And this is essentially what the free market system provides. The market is a natural device for the speedy conveyance of cheap, accurate and objective information. Since there is no absolute value in goods, the free market will tell you the exact going price and the level of demand of anything in any place and at any time within the society allowing it to function. It is speedy because the market functions around the clock all over the world, cheap because it is the free by-product of buying and selling, accurate because it is based upon an endless multiplicity of real transactions, and objective because the market is not an institution with a purpose or an ideology but a simple mirror of human desires in all their nakedness."

[5] Friedman, *Free,* 14.

[6] Kirk, *New World Coming* (London: Hodder and Stoughton, 1984), 116, would vehemently disagree with my perspective. "Until the unemployed are motivated sufficiently to mobilize themselves as a group to demand job opportunities as a fundamental right, there will be no significant change in the situation." Note, however, that he never asks, "What are these people to do?" nor "Who will pay them?" Gilder, *Wealth and Poverty,* 31, has a much more practical suggestion. "Are [capitalists] greedier than doctors or writers or professors of sociology or assistant secretaries of energy or commissars of wheat? Yes, their goals seem more mercenary. But this is only because money is their very means of production. Just as the sociologist requires books and free time and the bureaucrat needs arbitrary power, the capitalist needs capital. It is no more sensible to begrudge the entrepreneur his profits—or ascribe them to overweening avarice—than to begrudge the writer or professor his free time and access to libraries and research aids, or the scientist his laboratory and assistants, or the doctor his power to prescribe medicines and perform surgery. Capitalists need capital to fulfill their role in launching and financing enterprise. Are they self-interested? Presumably. But the crucial fact about them is

their deep interest and engagement in the world beyond themselves, impelled by their imagination, optimism and faith. The rewards of capitalists, however, do not simply constitute a tribute to virtue or an accommodation for a particular style of professional life. Entrepreneurs must be allowed to retain wealth for the practical reasons that only they, collectively, can possibly know where it should go, to whom it should be given."

[7] See Peter L. Berger, *The Capitalist Revolution* (New York: Basic Books, 1986) for an excellent discussion of the distinction between command economies and the welfare state version of a market economy.

[8] Novak, *Spirit*, 83.

[9] Joseph A. Schumpeter, *Capitalism, Socialism and Democracy* (New York: Harper and Row, 1976). This remains the classic discussion of socialism.

[10] For a careful defense of the communist perspective, see: Leo Huberman and Paul M. Sweezy, *Introduction to Socialism* (New York: Monthly Review, 1968) and Paul M. Sweezy, *The Theory of Capitalist Development: Principles of Marxian Political Economy* (New York: Monthly Review, 1970).

[11] See Sweezy, *Capitalist Development*, 59–66 and Robert L. Heilbroner, *The World Philosophers* (New York: Simon and Schuster, 1980), 153. This perspective can be seen in some Christian writers. Jacques Ellul, *Money and Power* (Downers Grove, Ill.: InterVarsity Press, 1984), 103, writes, "Next, the worker must be paid his whole salary; that is, a sum that really corresponds with his production and not one that is more or less arbitrarily fixed in a more or less free contract where the boss (whether an individual or the state) holds the advantage. This implies the disappearance of profit." Kirk, *New World*, 44, seems to agree when he says, "Every person has a right to develop himself freely and enjoy the fruit of his work. The present capitalist system is incompatible with these goals, because working people are used as mere instruments to produce wealth for another's pleasure. The worker, because he does not own what he produces, is alienated from himself as a person who creates." It is worth noting here that the theme of alienation is closely associated with contemporary Marxist criticism of capitalism.

[12] Sider, *Rich Christians in an Age of Hunger* (Downers Grove, Ill.: InterVarsity Press, 1984), 54.

## CHAPTER 7. ALTERNATIVE ECONOMIC SYSTEMS: AN EVALUATION

[1] "Pricing for Efficiency," *World Development Report 1983* (New York: Oxford University Press), 57–63, provides a wealth of informa-

tion that shows how government attempts to control economic growth in Third World countries have most often hindered the process.

[2] Bauer, *Equality: The Third World and Economic Delusion* (Cambridge: Harvard University Press, 1981), 17, provides an interesting parallel case. "A neat example of this process emerged in an American university. The students demanded much greater equality in all walks of life, including the grading of their papers. In response to these demands the teacher announced that from a given date the students would be given equal grades for their weekly papers, and that the grades would be based on the average performance of the class. The experiment brought about a rapid decline in average performance and thus in the average grade, because the incentive to work declined greatly."

[3] Note again that my defense of capitalism as an economic system does not imply approval of right-wing, repressive governments in Central and South America. As Michael Novak pointed out in *Will It Liberate?* (New York: Paulist Press, 1986), these countries, with their lack of political freedom, should not be considered capitalist in the proper sense.

## CHAPTER 8. UNDERSTANDING THE BIBLICAL VOCABULARY

[1] *Los Angeles Daily News,* March 19, 1986, 8.

[2] Wallis, *Agenda for Biblical People* (New York: Harper and Row, 1976), 3, argues "That God is on the side of the poor and that the Scriptures are uncompromising in their demand for economic and social justice is much more clear biblically than most of the issues over which churches have divided. The Scriptures claim that to know God is to do justice and to plead the cause of the oppressed." However, Wallis seems to have forgotten that oppression is only one of the causes of poverty. God may indeed be on the side of the poor who are oppressed, but Scripture certainly does not picture God as "on the side of" the poor who are slothful.

[3] Sider, *Rich Christians in an Age of Hunger* (Downers Grove, Ill.: InterVarsity Press, 1984), 104, 115, is particularly guilty of misusing the words *just* and *justice*. He insists, for example, that the poor have the right to make a "just" living without explaining how justice would work in that context. And he makes the wholly unjustified claim that "Justice . . . means massive economic sharing."

[4] The Bible does not address the matter of unjust social structures; that is a contemporary concern. To deal with this, we must apply biblical principles to issues of social structure and policy.

## CHAPTER 9. THE RICH AND THE POOR: RIGHTS AND RESPONSIBILITIES

[1] Wallis, *Agenda for Biblical People* (New York: Harper and Row, 1976), 90.

[2] Ellul, *Money and Power* (Downers Grove, Ill.: InterVarsity Press, 1984), 35.

## CHAPTER 10. ECONOMIC PERSPECTIVES ON JUSTICE AND OPPRESSION

[1] See Leftwich, *The Price System and Resource Allocation* (Hinsdale, Ill.: Dryden Press, 1979), and Robert Flanagan, Robert S. Smith, and Roland G. Ehrenberg, *Labor Economics and Labor Relations* (New York: Scott Foresman, 1984) for a standard presentation of the ideas summarized in this section.

[2] Gerald M. Meier, ed., *Leading Issues in Economic Development* (New York: Oxford University Press, 1976), 27, says, "The relationship between levels of economic development and the equity of income distribution is shown to be asymmetrically U-shaped, with more egalitarian income distributions being characteristic of both extreme economic underdevelopment and high levels of economic development. Between these extremes, however, the relationships are, for the most part, inverse: up to a point, higher rates of industrialization, faster increases in agricultural productivity, and high rates of growth all tend to shift the income distribution in favor of the higher-income groups and against the low-income groups." David Morawetz, *Twenty-five Years of Economic Development: 1950 to 1975* (Baltimore: The Johns Hopkins University Press, 1977), 38–39, makes the same point.

[3] See Sider, *Rich Christians in an Age of Hunger* (Downers Grove, Ill.: InterVarsity Press, 1984), 17, and Kirk, *New World Coming* (London: Hodder and Stoughton, 1984), 63–64.

[4] Sider, *Rich Christians,* 202, says, "Three things need to be done in the short run. First, developed nations should drastically reduce or eliminate trade barriers on imports from the [less developed countries]. Second, commodity prices need to be stabilized to avoid wild, short-term fluctuations. Third, we must deal with the problem that some commodities exported by Third World nations have experienced a long-term decline of relative prices." The first suggestion makes good economic sense, but probably cannot happen soon in the United States for political reasons. The last two suggestions show serious confusion about how commodity prices work.

[5] See Bauer, *Equality: The Third World and Economic Delusion* (Cambridge: Harvard University Press, 1981), 69, 77.

## CHAPTER 11. THE ETHICS OF AFFLUENCE

[1] I find the balance between love and realism displayed in Lewis Smedes, *Love Within Limits* (Grand Rapids: William B. Eerdmans, 1978) to be very helpful. Chapter 13, "Love Endures All Things" is particularly helpful when addressing the issues raised in this chapter.

[2] See William Diehl, *Thank God It's Monday!* (Philadelphia: Fortress Press, 1973) and John V. Hunter, *Enough is Enough* (Kingwood, Tex.: Hunter Books, 1984).

## APPENDIX.

[1] See also Kirk, *New World Coming* (London: Hodder and Stoughton, 1984); Ronald J. Sider, *Living More Simply* (Downers Grove, Ill.: InterVarsity Press, 1980); Simon, *Bread for the World* (Paulist Press and William B. Eerdmans, 1975); Sine, *The Mustard Seed Conspiracy* (Waco, Tex.: Word Books, 1981); Wallis, *Agenda for Biblical People* (New York: Harper and Row, 1976).

[2] Sider, *Rich Christians in an Age of Hunger* (Downers Grove, Ill.: InterVarsity Press, 1984), 65.

[3] See chapters 3, 8, 9.

[4] Sider, *Rich Christians*, 74. Wallis, *Agenda*, 27, is also prone to this interpretive blunder. "The biblical witness to the conversion of Zacchaeus shows that his repenting of sin and turning to Jesus involved making *reparations to the poor*. Because we profit from oppressive economic structures and relationships, the affluent countries are nations of rich young rulers and publicans who have robbed the poor."

[5] Sider, *Rich Christians*, 79, 90.

[6] Ibid., 96.

[7] Ibid., 22, 35. See also Sine, *Mustard Seed*, 20.

[8] Sider, *Rich Christians*, 86.

[9] Ibid., 172.

[10] Ibid., 95, 113.

[11] Ibid., 112.

[12] See Gloria Copeland, *God's Will Is Prosperity* (Fort Worth, Tex.: KCP Publications, 1978); Kenneth Copeland, *The Laws of Prosperity* (Fort Worth, Tex.: KCP Publications, 1974); Charles Hunter, *God's Conditions for Prosperity* (Kingwood, Tex.: Hunter Books, 1984); Elbert Willis, *God's Plan for Financial Prosperity* (Lafayette, Louisiana: Fill the Gap Publications, 1975).

[13] Bronislaw Malinowski, *Magic, Science, and Religion and Other Essays* (1948; reprint ed., Westport, Conn.: Greenwood Press, 1984).

[14] K. Copeland, *Laws*, 26. See also Vernard Eller, *The Simple Life* (Grand Rapids: William B. Eerdmans, 1973), 122.

[15] G. Copeland, *God's Will*, 25.

[16] Willis, *God's Plan*, 29. See also G. Copeland, *God's Will*, 47ff.

[17] G. Copeland, *God's Will*, 70ff.

[18] Chilton, David, *Productive Christians and an Age of Guilt Manipulators: A Biblical Response to Ronald S. Sider,* 2d ed. (Tyler, Tex.: Institute for Christian Economics, 1982), 39.

[19] Ibid., 20.

[20] Thomas S. Kuhn, *The Structure of Scientific Revolutions,* Foundations of the Unity of Science Series, vol. 2, no. 2 (Chicago, Ill.: University of Chicago Press, 1970).

[21] Chilton, *Productive Christians,* 24.

# BIBLIOGRAPHY

## 1. Christian Reflection

Barron, Bruce. *The Health and Wealth Gospel: What's Going on Today in a Movement that Has Shaped the Faith of Millions?* Downers Grove: InterVarsity Press, 1987.

*A balanced, fair appraisal of the theological position that asserts that the gospel promises health and wealth.*

Berkhof, Hendrik. *Christ and the Powers.* Scottdale, Pa.: Herald Press, 1962.

*The classical biblical theology of the powers.*

Bulle, Florence. *"God Wants You Rich" and Other Enticing Doctrines.* Minneapolis: Bethany House Publishers, 1983.

Burkett, Larry. *Your Finances in Changing Times.* Chicago: Moody Press, 1982.

*A balanced, thoughtful approach to Christian financial planning.*

Butler, Stuart, and Anna Kondratas. *Out of the Poverty Trap: A Conservative Strategy for Welfare Reform.* New York: Macmillan, 1987.

*An attempt to develop a positive approach to welfare reform which begins from the premise that the current situation is seriously deficient.*

Campolo, Tony. "Conversion and Wealth." *World Christian* (January/February, 1986): 36–37.

*A brief article that points out that conversion does lead to prosperity in the presence of political freedom. Campolo argues, however, that it may take political action to create an environment that will allow for such freedom.*

Chilton, David. *Productive Christians and an Age of Guilt Manipulators: A Biblical Response to Ronald J. Sider.* 2d ed. with a preface by Gary North. Tyler, Tex.: Institute for Christian Economics, 1982.

*A response to Ron Sider written with an abrasive style. Nonetheless, a book worth considering.*

Clapp, Rodney. "Democracy as Heresy." *Christianity Today* (February 20, 1987): 17–23.

*A study of the recent Reconstructionist movement; it focuses on G. Bahnsen, Gary North, and R. J. Rushdoony.*

Clouse, Robert G., ed. *Wealth and Poverty: Four Christian Views of Economics.* Downers Grove, Ill.: InterVarsity Press, 1984.

*Includes: William E. Diehl, "The Guided-Market System"; Art Gish, "Decentralist Economics"; John Gladwin, "Centralist Economics"; Gary North, "Free Market Capitalism."*

Copeland, Gloria. *God's Will Is Prosperity.* Fort Worth, Tex.: Kenneth Copeland Publications, 1978.

*A popular book from the Charismatic perspective; it presents the view that the Atonement provides health and prosperity as well as redemption.*

Copeland, Kenneth. *The Laws of Prosperity.* Fort Worth, Tex.: Kenneth Copeland Publications, 1974.

*Takes the same perspective as the book by Gloria Copeland.*

DeVos, Richard M. with Charles Paul Conn. *Believe!* Old Tappan, N.J.: Fleming H. Revell, 1975.

*An inspirational book that argues for Christian involvement in the business world.*

Diehl, William E. *Thank God. It's Monday!* Philadelphia: Fortress Press, 1973.

*A positive statement of the "theology of enough."*

Eller, Vernard. *The Simple Life: The Christian Stance toward Possessions.* Grand Rapids: William B. Eerdmans, 1973.

*Argues that Christian simplicity is primarily keeping the kingdom of God and that the quality of consumption is not relevant.*

Ellul, Jacques. *Money and Power*. Downers Grove, Ill.: InterVarsity Press, 1984.

*A study arguing that money is one of the principalities and powers; since the powers are fallen, money can enslave.*

Farah, Charles, Jr. *From the Pinnacle of the Temple*. Plainfield, N.J.: Logos International, n.d.

*Argues against the "name it and claim it" theological perspective; cover carries the subtitle: "Faith or Presumption?"*

Foster, Richard J. *Money, Sex and Power: The Challenge of the Disciplined Life*. New York: Harper & Row, 1985.

*Presents one of the more balanced perspectives on money.*

Gaebelein, Frank E. "Old Testament Foundations for Living More Simply." In *Living More Simply*, edited by Ronald J. Sider. Downers Grove, Ill.: InterVarsity Press, 1980.

Goba, Bonganjola. "Contextual Understanding: The Problem in S.A. of Differing Perceptions and Analyses." *Transformation* 3:2 (April/June 1986): 17–20.

Griffiths, Brian. *The Creation of Wealth*. London: Hodder and Stoughton, 1984.

*A study of how wealth is created.*

————. *Morality and the Market Place*. London: Hodder and Stoughton, 1982.

*A thoughtful argument to show that Christianity and capitalism are compatible.*

Halteman, Jim. *Market Capitalism and Christianity* Grand Rapids: Baker, 1988.

*A thoughtful Anabaptist response to market capitalism by a Christian economics professor.*

Hunter, Charles. *God's Conditions for Prosperity*. Kingwood, Tex.: Hunter Books, 1984.

*Defends the position that God wants all Christians to be prosperous.*

Kirk, J. Andrew. *A New World Coming: A Fresh Look at the Gospel for Today*. London: Hodder and Stoughton, 1984.

*A strong indictment of the current economic order by a British evangelical.*

Kraft, Charles. *Christianity in Culture*. New York: Orbis, 1979.

———. "Contextualization of Theology." *Evangelical Missions Quarterly* 14 (1978): 31–36.

———. "Interpreting in a Cultural Context." *Journal of the Evangelical Society* 21:4 (December 1978): 357–67.

Mullin, Redmond. *The Wealth of Christians*. Maryknoll, N.Y.: Orbis Books, 1984.

*A study of how Christians have dealt with the question of riches throughout church history.*

Nash, Ronald H. *Poverty and Wealth: The Christian Debate over Capitalism*. Westchester, Ill.: Crossway Books, 1986.

*An informal introduction to economics by an evangelical.*

Nicholls, Bruce J. *Contextualization: A Theology of Gospel and Culture*. Downers Grove, Ill.: InterVarsity, 1979.

Novak, Michael. "Democratic Capitalism." *Transformation* 2:1 (January/March, 1985): 18–23.

———. *The Spirit of Democratic Capitalism*. New York: Simon and Schuster, 1982.

*A powerful defense of capitalism by a noted Catholic theologian.*

———. *Toward a Theology of the Corporation*. Washington: American Enterprise Institute for Public Policy Research, 1981.

———. "Why Latin American Is Poor." *Atlantic Monthly* (March, 1982): 66–75.

———. *Will It Liberate? Questions About Liberation Theology*. New York: Paulist Press, 1986.

Perkins, John. *Let Justice Role Down*. Glendale, Calif.: Regal Books, 1976.

*An action plan for Christian involvement in social change.*

———. *A Quiet Revolution: The Christian Response to Human Need, A Strategy for Today*. Waco, Tex.: Word Books, 1976.

*The story of the Voice of Calvary ministry in Mississippi.*

————. *With Justice for All*. Glendale, Calif: Regal Books, 1982.

Schaible, Cynthia R. "The Gospel of the Good Life." *Eternity* (February, 1981): 20–27.

   *A short evaluation of the position that God wants Christians to be successful and prosperous.*

Scholssberg, Herbert. *Idols for Destruction: Christian Faith and Its Confrontation with American Society*. Nashville: Thomas Nelson, 1983.

Sider, Ronald J., ed. *Cry Justice: The Bible Speaks on Hunger and Poverty*. Downers Grove, Ill: InterVarsity Press, 1980.

   *A collection of biblical passages on the poor with comments.*

————. *Living More Simply: Biblical Principles and Practical Models*. Downers Grove, Ill.: InterVarsity Press, 1980.

————. *Rich Christians in an Age of Hunger*. Rev. ed. Downers Grove, Ill.: InterVarsity Press, 1984.

   *A call for Christian involvement in the problems of world hunger.*

Simon, Arthur. *Bread for the World*. Paulist Press and William B. Eerdmans, 1975.

   *The reflections of an evangelical social activist on issues relating to hunger.*

Sine, Tom. *The Mustard Seed Conspiracy*. Waco, Tex.: Word Books, 1981.

Smedes, Lewis B. *Love Within Limits: A Realist's View of 1 Corinthians 13*. Grand Rapids: William B. Eerdmans, 1978.

   *Devotional reflections on the "love" chapter.*

Stringfellow, William. *An Ethic for Christians and Other Aliens in a Strange Land*. Waco, Tex.: Word Books, 1973.

Taylor, John V. *Enough Is Enough: A Biblical Call for Moderation in a Consumer-Oriented Society*. Minneapolis: Augsburg, 1975.

Wallis, Jim. *Agenda for Biblical People*. New York: Harper and Row, 1976.

   *A passionate call for evangelical social action.*

White, John. *The Golden Cow: Materialism in the Twentieth Century Church*. Downers Grove, Ill.: InterVarsity Press, 1979.

*A balanced work which recognizes the value of God's creation and the danger of materialism.*

Willis, Elbert. *God's Plan for Financial Prosperity*. Lafayette, La.: Fill the Gap Publications, 1975.

*A short popular study guide based on the author's cassette tapes.*

Wolterstorff, Nicholas. *Until Justice and Peace Embrace*. Grand Rapids: William B. Eerdmans, 1983.

Yancey, Philip. "Learning to Live with Money." *Christianity Today* (December 14, 1984): 30–42.

Yoder, John Howard. *The Politics of Jesus*. Grand Rapids: Eerdmans, 1972.

*A classic and provocative study of the Gospels from a Mennonite position.*

## 2. Economic Texts

Bauer, P. T. *Dissent on Development*. Rev. ed. Cambridge: Harvard University Press, 1976.

*A powerful argument against attempts to circumvent natural market forces.*

_____. *Equality: The Third World and Economic Delusion*. Cambridge: Harvard University Press, 1981.

*Continues the argument of his previous book.*

Berger, Peter L. *The Capitalist Revolution: Fifty Propositions about Prosperity, Equity, and Liberty*. New York: Basic Books, 1986.

*A reasoned defense of capitalism from the perspective of a sociologist.*

_____. "Death Aid." *Wall Street Journal*. (June 27, 1986): 26.

Blinder, Alan S. *Hard Heads, Soft Hearts: Tough Minded Economics for a Just Society*. Reading, Mass.: Addison Wesley. 1987.

*An excellent attempt by a moderate democratic economist to respond to social needs (education, employment, and the environment) without transgressing accepted economic conclusions.*

"Christian Faith and Economics." *Transformation* 4 (June–Sept./Oct.–Dec. 1987): 3–4.

*A special double issue of the journal which includes articles by Sir Frederick Catherwood, Samuel Escobar, Nicholas Wolterstorff, Herbert Schlossberg, Stephen Mott, Uto Middelmann, and Peter Hill.*

Dornbusch, Rudiger and Stanley Fischer. *Macro-Economics.* 2d ed. New York: McGraw-Hill, 1981.

*A standard text.*

Ekelund, Robert B., Jr., and Robert F. Hebert. *A History of Economic Theory and Method.* New York: McGraw-Hill, 1983.

Ethier, Wilfred. *Modern International Economics.* New York: W. W. Norton, 1983.

*A standard text in international economics.*

Flanagan, Robert I., Robert S. Smith, and Roland G. Ehrenberg. *Labor Economics and Labor Relations.* New York: Scott Foresman, 1984.

*A standard text.*

Friedman, Milton and Rose Friedman. *Free to Choose: A Personal Statement.* New York: Avon Books, 1980.

*A passionate defense of the free-market perspective.*

Gilder, George. *Wealth and Poverty.* New York: Bantam Books, 1981.

*A popular statement of the conservative position in economics.*

Heilbroner, Robert L. *The Worldly Philosophers.* 5th ed. New York: Simon and Schuster, 1980.

*A popular, well-written history of economic theory.*

Huberman, Leo and Paul M. Sweezy. *Introduction to Socialism.* Modern Reader Paperbacks, 1968.

*A defense of Marxism.*

Johnson, Paul. "Movement in the Market: Mobility and Economics in the Free Society." In *On Freedom: Essays from the Frankfurt Conference,* edited by John A. Howard with a foreword by Robert A. Nisbet. Greenwich, Conn.: Devin-Adair, 1984.

Leftwich, Richard H. *The Price System and Resource Allocation.* 7th ed. Hinsdale, Ill.: Dryden Press, 1979.

*A standard text in microeconomics.*

Lichtheim, George. *Marxism: An Historical and Critical Study.* New York: Columbia University Press, 1964.

Meier, Gerald M., ed. *Leading Issues in Economic Development.* 3d ed. New York: Oxford University Press, 1976.

*A collection of essays on development.*

Morawetz, David. *Twenty-five Years of Economic Development: 1950 to 1975.* Baltimore: Johns Hopkins University Press, 1977.

*Includes a great deal of helpful statistical data on development.*

Schumacher, E. F. *Small Is Beautiful: Economics as If People Mattered.* New York: Harper and Row, 1973.

Schumpeter, Joseph A. *Capitalism, Socialism and Democracy.* New York: Harper and Row, 1976.

*The classical argument that society will move toward socialism.*

Stigler, Wilfred. *The Theory of Price.* 3d ed. New York: Macmillan, 1966.

*A standard text in microeconomics.*

Sweezy, Paul M. *The Theory of Capitalist Development: Principles of Marxian Political Economy.* Modern Reader Paperbacks, 1970.

*A standard defense of the Marxist perspective on economics. Wogaman, J. Philip. Economics and Ethics: A Christian Inquiry. Philadelphia: Fortress, 1986.*

*A thoughtful analysis of economic priorities.*

World Bank. *World Development Report, 1983.* New York: Oxford University Press.

*An invaluable source of data on the economic situation in each of the world's 100+ countries.*

# SUBJECT INDEX

Abundance, 30; just distribution of, 52, 103; relation to wealth, 21; thanksgiving for, 97–98; use of, 23

Adam, 16–17, 21

Affluence, Christian view of, 28, 90–100; definition of, 8. *See also* Wealth.

Africa, 81, 82

Agrarian society, 85–88

Alternative economic systems, evaluation of, 55–59; introduction to, 42–54

American wealth, 38–41

American welfare system, 98

Amos, 67, 69, 70

Asceticism, 14, 101–4

Barter system, 44

Bible, contextualization in, 12–13, 14, 115n.1; distortion of, 105; integration with world, 26–28; interpretation of, 12–15, 26; theology of, 13, 14, 15, 17; view of competition, 92; view of poor, 77; view of wealth, 62, 63, 64, 71–72, 105. *See also* Scripture.

Calculator, 34

Capital, 38, 41, 87

Capitalism, 44–45, 51–52, 55, 56–57; Christian, 93, 107, 110n.2; competition in, 92–93; critics of, 53, 110n.1; guided, 50, 59; laissez-faire, 50, 58, 81; relation to welfare state, 51, 59, 112n.7; theological evaluation of, 57, 84–85, 93; wages in, 84. *See also* Economic systems, Market system, Prices, Production.

Capitalists, 25, 45, 58, 107, 111n.6

Central America, 84

Chilton, David, 11, 106–8

China, 36, 37, 56, 58

Christianity, 45, 105

Christian(s), 58, 63, 69, 72; capitalists, 25, 45, 58, 107; employer, 95, 99; relation to the Third World, 68, 85, 89, 99, 100; responsibilities toward the poor or weak, 77, 93; socialists, 45, 110n.2; theology of enough, 97–98; use of time, 91

Church, 26, 40, 65, 76, 99, 100

Colonies and wealth, 39–40

Command economies, 44–45, 51–54. *See also* Government.

Commodities prices, 81, 88–89, 114n.4

Communism, 52–53, 112n.10

Compensation, 83, 94–96, 99

Competition, ethics of, 92–94

Computers, 34, 35, 50

Consumers, 5

Consumption, 46, 96–98

Copeland, Gloria, 105

Courts, 77

Covenant, 19–20, 101–2

Covetousness, 61, 65–66, 71–72

Creation, 16–17, 26; man's task in, 21–23; nature of, 18–19; purpose of, 19–21; worship of, 63

Cultural values, 36–37

125